Placebo Effects

Basic Mechanisms and Clinical Applications

Editors:
Regine Klinger
Luana Colloca

Zeitschrift für Psychologie

Vol. 222, No. 3, 2014

HOGREFE

Library of Congress Cataloging in Publication

is available via the Library of Congress Marc Database under the
LC Control Number 2014945018

PUBLISHING OFFICES
USA: Hogrefe Publishing, 38 Chauncy Street, Suite 1002, Boston, MA 02111
Phone (866) 823-4726, Fax (617) 354-6875, E-mail customerservice@hogrefe-publishing.com
EUROPE: Hogrefe Publishing, Merkelstr. 3, 37085 Göttingen, Germany
Phone +49 551 99950-0, Fax +49 551 99950-425, E-mail publishing@hogrefe.com

SALES & DISTRIBUTION
USA: Hogrefe Publishing, Customer Services Department, 30 Amberwood Parkway, Ashland,
OH 44805, Phone (800) 228-3749, Fax (419) 281-6883, E-mail customerservice@hogrefe.com
EUROPE: Hogrefe Publishing, Merkelstr. 3, 37085 Göttingen, Germany
Phone +49 551 99950-0, Fax +49 551 99950-425, E-mail publishing@hogrefe.com

OTHER OFFICES
CANADA: Hogrefe Publishing, 660 Eglinton Ave. East, Suite 119-514, Toronto, Ontario M4G 2K2
SWITZERLAND: Hogrefe Publishing, Länggass-Strasse 76, CH-3000 Bern 9

Hogrefe Publishing
Incorporated and registered in the Commonwealth of Massachusetts, USA, and in Göttingen, Lower Saxony, Germany

ISBN 978-0-88937-463-8

Contents

Editorial

Approaches to a Complex Phenomenon

The Basic Mechanisms and Clinical Applications of Placebo Effects

Regine Klinger[1] and Luana Colloca[2]

[1]Psychotherapeutic Outpatient Clinic, Department of Psychology, University of Hamburg, Germany,
[2]Department of Bioethics, Clinical Center, National Institutes of Health, Bethesda, MD, USA

There is probably no other human phenomenon that better reflects the inseparable interaction between psychological and somatic factors than the placebo effect. This phenomenon is a complex psychobiological process consisting of learning and expectancy components acting on neurophysiological systems, and its efficacy has been confirmed empirically in a range of fields such as pain and the immune system. Inert substances such as sugar pills can trigger placebo effects, and these effects can also enhance the response to active treatments.

This topical issue presents the complexity of the phenomenon called placebo effect. The articles included here describe different research approaches to the topic and look at different models and facets of the placebo phenomenon.

During the past decades the most impressive demonstrations of these effects have been presented in the field of pain and placebo analgesia. The effectiveness of analgesic placebo responses remains unchallenged and our knowledge about the underlying mechanisms that produce the placebo effect is expanding rapidly. Together with expectancy theories, classical conditioning has been discussed as being a major explanatory model. However, other learning principles, such as social learning (via vicarious reinforcement), are thought to play an important role in the development and maintenance of placebo analgesia. From a neurobiological viewpoint, research findings have revealed the involvement of cortical, subcortical, and recently spinal structures in the placebo-induced modulation of pain that cognitively triggers the release of endogenous opioid and non-opioid substances (Colloca, Klinger, Flor, & Bingel, 2013).

Insights into the underlying mechanisms and the neurobiological foundation (Colloca et al., 2013) of the analgesic placebo effect have now made it possible to develop principles for clinical application (Klinger, Colloca, Bingel, & Flor, 2014). These principles must, of course, be justifiable within ethical boundaries. In their article addressing this issue, Colloca, Jonas, Killen, Miller, and Shurtleff (2014) point out that, in the current state of medicine, there are numerous examples of inappropriate uses of placebos, often justified by the patient's urgency for help on the one hand, and the lack of appropriate medication on the other. The authors emphasize the need to focus on elements of the clinical encounter and the patient-physician relationship to increase the placebo effect. Clearly caution is necessary in harnessing placebo effects in medicine to treat patients while avoiding deception. Accordingly, the study of the placebo effect should be incorporated in the core clinical practice curriculum of all health practitioners.

Benedetti, Amanzio, and Maggi (1995) and Colloca, Lopiano, Lanotte, and Benedetti (2004) showed that pain treatments (e.g., opioids) consist of a verum component (active pharmacological component) and a placebo component. Regarding the latter, there are many contextual factors associated with the treatment, such as expectancy, fear, previous experiences with clinical staff, and co-interventions, but also illness-related factors and personality variables. It is necessary to boost these specific aspects systematically to ultimately enhance the analgesic effect. In Germany, for instance, this innovative thought has already been implemented in the S3 guidelines of the working group of scientific medical societies (Arbeitsgemeinschaft der Wissenschaftlichen Medizinischen Fachgesellschaften, AWMF – see http://www.awmf.org); this association represents Germany in the Council for International Organizations of Medical Sciences, CIOMS) for the "treatment

DOI: 10.1027/2151-2604/a000175

of acute and perioperative pain." It is recommended therein to use the potential of the placebo effect in the clinical context and to avoid nocebo effects (Klinger, Thomm, Bryant, & Becker, 2009). The placebo effect has thereby become more acceptable amongst health practitioners. It is important to note that the aim is explicitly not to replace effective pain medication with placebos but to recognize the placebo effect as an additive component that can optimize every pain medication beyond its pure pharmacology-based effectiveness. This paradigm shift toward the explicit use of the placebo effect offers a completely new opportunity for the prevention and treatment of chronic pain. Therefore, the clinical value of the placebo effect needs to be discussed with patients. This approach should involve using psychological strategies in assisting the patient to establish positive, yet realistic expectations regarding the medical pain treatment.

Placebo effects are highly specific. Finniss, Kaptchuk, Miller, and Benedetti (2010) described 12 different mechanisms of placebo effects. Keeping this in mind, one can think of the placebo effect as being a form of mimicry of bodily procedures caused by the medication. For example, analgesic placebos activate the endorphin system, and placebos used as Parkinson disease medication activate dopamine in the striatum and change the activity of neurons in the basal ganglia and the thalamus. However, a specific mechanism is not always detectable. The underlining placebo mechanisms of antidepressant drugs seem to be somewhat dubious. In his provocative paper on antidepressants and the placebo effect published in this issue, Kirsch (2014) shows that regardless of contradictory mechanisms of antidepressant medication, antidepressant placebos are almost as effective as antidepressants, yet eliciting far fewer side effects.

Vase, Skyt, Petersen, and Price (2014) review placebo and nocebo effects in chronic pain patients and reveal the influence of expectations and emotions on the experience of pain. In a further review, Sölle, Bartholomäus, Worm, and Klinger (2014) show how classical conditioning and expectancy produce placebo effects with itching. Vits and Schedlowski (2014) review the current literature about learned placebo effects in the immune system.

Carlino, Benedetti, and Pollo (2014) focus on placebo effects on physical performance and show how it can be can manipulated via verbal suggestions, whilst Geers, Rose, Fowler, and Brown (2014) look at patient involvement in treatment decision-making and show that, depending on patients' prior experience with treatments, this involvement can enhance or hinder placebo effects, respectively. Hofmann, Wrobel, Kessner, and Bingel (2014) demonstrate that carry-over effects after treatment failure can be minimized by changing the route of application, for example, a pill replaced by a cream. Kamping, Müller, Klinger, Schmitz, and Flor (2014) also focus on chronic pain patients. They consider the influence of attitude, experience, and expectation on the placebo effect and present an instrument to assess both specific attitudes toward pain medication and experiences with pain medication.

The similarity between pain and itching sensations suggests a transfer of the placebo analgesic effect to anti-itching medication. Finally, the current state of placebo research holds sufficient evidence for careful considerations of clinical implications of placebo effects. Employing the placebo effect according to its mechanisms and strictly following the underlying mechanisms in the development and the maintenance of the placebo effect is required.

References

Benedetti, F., Amanzio, M., & Maggi, G. (1995). Potentiation of placebo analgesia by proglumide. *Lancet, 346*, 1231.

Carlino, E., Benedetti, F., & Pollo, A. (2014). The effects of manipulating verbal suggestions on physical performance. *Zeitschrift für Psychologie, 222*, 154–164. doi: 10.1027/2151-2604/a000178

Colloca, L., Jonas, W. B., Killen, J., Miller, F. G., & Shurtleff, D. (2014). Reevaluating the placebo effect in medical practice. *Zeitschrift für Psychologie, 222*, 124–127. doi: 10.1027/2151-2604/a000177

Colloca, L., Klinger, R., Flor, H., & Bingel, U. (2013). Placebo analgesia: Psychological and neurobiological mechanisms. *Pain, 154*, 511–514.

Colloca, L., Lopiano, L., Lanotte, M., & Benedetti, F. (2004). Overt versus covert treatment for pain, anxiety, and Parkinson's disease. *Lancet Neurology, 3*, 679–684.

Finniss, D. G., Kaptchuk, T. J., Miller, F., & Benedetti, F. (2010). Biological, clinical, and ethical advances of placebo effects. *Lancet, 375*, 686–695.

Geers, A. L., Rose, J. P., Fowler, S. L., & Brown, J. A. (2014). Patient involvement in treatment decision making can help or hinder placebo analgesia: The moderating role of prior experience. *Zeitschrift für Psychologie, 222*, 165–170. doi: 10.1027/2151-2604/a000179

Hofmann, M., Wrobel, N., Kessner, S., & Bingel, U. (2014). Minimizing carry-over effects after treatment failure and maximizing therapeutic outcome: Can changing the route of administration mitigate the influence of treatment history? *Zeitschrift für Psychologie, 222*, 171–178. doi: 10.1027/2151-2604/a000180

Kamping, S., Müller, M., Klinger, R., Schmitz, J., & Flor, H. (2014). Analgesics in chronic back pain: The significance of patient attitudes to them and prior experience with them for placebo responses. *Zeitschrift für Psychologie, 222*, 179–185. doi: 10.1027/2151-2604/a000182

Kirsch, I. (2014). Antidepressants and the placebo effect. *Zeitschrift für Psychologie, 222*, 128–134. doi: 10.1027/2151-2604/a000176

Klinger, R., Colloca, L., Bingel, U., & Flor, H. (2014). Placebo analgesia: Clinical applications. *Pain, 155*, 1055–1058. Advance online publication. doi: 10.1016/j.pain.2013.12.007

Klinger, R, Thomm, M., Bryant, M., & Becker, M. (2009). Patienteninformation und -aufklärung [Patient information and education]. In H. Laubenthal, M. Becker, S. Sauerland, & E. Neugebauer (Eds.), *Deutsche interdisziplinäre Vereinigung für Schmerztherapie (DIVS). S3-Leitlinie Behandlung akuter und perioperativer posttraumatischer Schmerzen* (pp. 19–22) AWMF-Reg.-Nr. 041/001. Cologne, Germany: Deutscher Ärzte-Verlag.

Sölle, A., Bartholomäus, T., Worm, M., & Klinger, R. (2014). How to psychologically minimize scratching impulses: Benefits of placebo effects on itching using classical conditioning and expectancy. *Zeitschrift für Psychologie, 222*, 140–147. doi: 10.1027/2151-2604/a000183

Vase, L., Skyt, I., Petersen, G. L., & Price, D. D. (2014). Placebo and nocebo effects in chronic pain patients: How expectations and emotions contribute to the experience of pain. *Zeitschrift für Psychologie, 222*, 135–139. doi: 10.1027/2151-2604/a000181

Vits, S., & Schedlowski, M. (2014). Learned placebo effects in the immune system. *Zeitschrift für Psychologie, 222*, 148–153. doi: 10.1027/2151-2604/a000184

Regine Klinger

Department of Psychology
Outpatient Clinic of Behavior Therapy
University of Hamburg
Von-Melle-Park 5
20146 Hamburg
Germany
Tel. +49 40 42838-5374
Fax +49 40 42838-8008
E-mail rklinger@uni-hamburg.de

Review Article

Reevaluating the Placebo Effect in Medical Practice

Luana Colloca,[1,2,3] Wayne B. Jonas,[4] John Killen Jr.,[1] Franklin G. Miller,[3] and David Shurtleff[1]

[1]National Center for Complementary and Alternative Medicine (NCCAM), Bethesda, MD, USA, [2]National Institute of Mental Health (NIMH), Bethesda, MD, USA, [3]Clinical Center, Department of Bioethics, National Institutes of Health, Bethesda, MD, USA, [4]Samueli Institute, Alexandria, VA, USA

Abstract. Recent findings from placebo research corroborate the evidence that the placebo effect represents a promising model to shed new light on brain-mind-body interactions. In particular, this research has partially elucidated the role of how patients' expectations and the quality of physician-patient communication can influence the efficacy of interventions and overall clinical outcomes. Accordingly, the study of the placebo effect should be incorporated in the core clinical practice curriculum of all health practitioners. While the growing knowledge about the placebo effect points to it being an irreducible primary reality of medical practice, an ethical analysis aimed at avoiding the misuse of *placebos* and maximizing beneficial *placebo effects* is needed.

Keywords: placebo, expectations, ethics, policy, patient-clinician communication

The placebo effect is a well-recognized and clinically-important phenomenon in medicine. Over the past several years there has been considerable research in elucidating the mechanisms underlying the placebo effect (Colloca, Klinger, Flor, & Bingel, 2013; Colloca & Miller, 2013; Enck, Bingel, Schedlowski, & Rief, 2013; Meissner et al., 2011). In particular this research has elucidated understanding of the role of how patients' expectations and the quality of physician-patient communication can influence the efficacy of an intervention (Bingel et al., 2011; Colloca & Finniss, 2012; Colloca, Lopiano, Lanotte, & Benedetti, 2004). In addition, a more complete understanding of these psychobiological effects may help investigators to better detect intervention-specific effects, and help clinicians to optimize patients' adherence and response to therapeutic regimens, thereby leading to even greater efficacy of treatment (Klinger, Colloca, Bingel, & Flor, 2014).

Here we discuss some implications of current research on physicians' use of placebos as they seek to balance patients' desires and demands, while also maximizing the opportunity for beneficial placebo effects. We also emphasize the need for better evidence on the safety and true relative effectiveness of placebos and placebo effects in clinical practice.

For the purposes of this article, we use the term "*placebo*" to describe simulated medical treatments – that is, interventions which lack pharmacological or physiological properties that lead to specific efficacy in treating a specific patient's condition. Conversely, when we use the term "*placebo effect*," we are focusing on various measurable psychobiological phenomena resulting from expectations that a treatment will be effective.

Examples of Placebo Effects in Laboratory Encounters

Recent research involving clinical investigations and state-of-the-art neuroimaging techniques has unearthed a number of important findings regarding mechanisms of placebo effects that are not necessarily related to the administration of any placebos (Colloca et al., 2004; Enck et al., 2013). The study of the placebo effect is increasingly being framed as the investigation of the psychosocial context and inner factors surrounding the patient and any medical treatments, and the effect of this context on the patient's mind, brain and body when one expects a therapeutic benefit (Colloca, Klinger, et al., 2013; Di Blasi & Reilly, 2005).

Placebo effects are formed through verbal anticipations of benefits, learning mechanisms and patient-clinician interactions (Colloca, Klinger, et al., 2013). After repetitive administrations of an efficacious painkiller paired with a placebo, the placebo alone is capable of inducing conditioned responses similar to those of the active drug. Verbal suggestions of therapeutic benefit by clinicians can also trigger placebo effects. Moreover, expectation of symptomatic relief can be created by the observation of a benefit in another person and by interpersonal interactions.

In sum, when triggered by the appropriate environmental signals, placebos can produce clinically meaningful symptomatic relief for a wide variety of medical conditions (Benedetti, 2008; Colloca & Milller, 2013; Klinger et al., 2014).

For example, Linde et al. reported that patients with higher expectations regarding acupuncture's efficacy, showed higher benefit than those with low expectations, suggesting that patients' beliefs can dramatically shape reported outcomes (Linde, Fassler, & Meissner, 2011). Similarly, in patients with Parkinson's disease, the perceived treatment assignment had more impact on motor function improvement and quality of life than the actual surgical treatment -real or sham human embryonic dopamine neuron implantation (McRae et al., 2004). These (and other recent) studies indicate that patient expectations have an impact on relief of symptoms and quality of life thus indicating that patients' preferences should be taken into account when equivalent therapeutic strategies are available.

On the other hand it is critical to emphasize that current evidence suggests that expectations and placebo effects influence primarily subjective symptoms, and evidence that they can influence the pathophysiology of serious diseases is scant. An interesting recent study clearly illustrates the lack of evidence about the influences of the placebo effect on serious diseases (Wechsler et al., 2011). Asthmatic patients were randomized to receive an albuterol inhaler, a placebo inhaler, sham acupuncture, or no intervention and subjective measures of asthma and pulmonary functions were evaluated. Patients' reports of improvement were 50% after the albuterol inhaler, 45% after the placebo inhaler, and 46% after the sham acupuncture and the three interventions were significantly greater than the no-intervention control (21%). However, pulmonary functions improved under albuterol active treatment only as compared with the placebo interventions, suggesting a substantial difference between patient's needs and satisfaction and therapeutic effects (Wechsler et al., 2011).

A Controversial Use of Placebos in Medical Practice

Despite the recent advances in mechanistic and translational research, placebos are used in daily clinical practice often in an inappropriate fashion. A recent systematic review of twenty-two cross-sectional, qualitative, and longitudinal studies investigating frequency of placebo use among health care professionals from twelve countries indicated that the prevalence of placebo use in clinical practice ranged from 17 to 80% among physicians and from 51 to 100% among nurses (Fassler, Meissner, Schneider, & Linde, 2010). In particular, 46% of a random sample of 1,200 internists and rheumatologists in the United States reported recommending an intervention "primarily to enhance patient expectation," at least 2–3 times per month. Only 5% reported using pure placebos, such as sugar pills and saline injections; others recommended using over-the-counter analgesics, vitamins, sedatives, and antibiotics (Tilburt, Emanuel, Kaptchuk, Curlin, & Miller, 2008).

In Denmark, 503 physicians including general practitioners, hospital-based clinicians and private specialists engaged in the use of antibiotics, physiotherapy, sedatives, or vitamins prescribed as placebos "to follow the wish of the patient and avoid conflict" (Hrobjartsson & Norup, 2003).

In Germany, when asked about the placebo use, 208 general practitioners reported that they used a placebo at least once in their practice; 45% used placebos, such as saline injections and sugar pills, at least once per year and 76% of general practitioners used medical interventions that have pharmacological or physical activity but have no intrinsic effect on the patient's disease or symptoms. The rationale for the use of placebo was to elicit "a psychological effect, followed by the expectation of patients to receive a treatment" (Meissner, Hofner, Fassler, & Linde, 2012).

In the United Kingdom, 782 general practitioners indicated that 12% of general practitioners used placebos while 97% used active treatments given as placebos at least once in their careers; 1% of respondents used placebos, and 77% used active treatments (e.g., antibiotics, vitamins, probiotics, and subclinical doses of otherwise effective therapies) as placebos at least once per week (Howick et al., 2013).

Of particular concern is the prescription of drugs that are not medically indicated, with little likelihood of actual benefit but potentially serious side effects. This practice raises many serious medical and ethical concerns, most notably serious side effects, unjustifiable rationale, and lack of a plausible motivation (Miller & Colloca, 2009). The prescription of such placebo interventions is generally associated with a deceptive or *opaque* disclosure although, the general belief that deception is necessary to induce placebo effects has been challenged. In fact, an open-label study showed that placebos induced improvement of symptoms in patients with Irritable Bowel Syndrome who were explicitly instructed to take placebos, described as pills without medication, with the purpose to evoke a placebo effect (Kaptchuk et al., 2010). This observation suggests that patients can develop placebo effects from a simulated medical intervention even when transparently informed. While additional research is needed to confirm or elaborate on the perspective of open-label placebos, their prescription may put physicians in an uncomfortable position. Physicians should not give placebos deceptively but should understand how placebo mechanisms can be activated when valid therapies are given to patients (Colloca & Miller, 2011; Klinger et al., 2014; Miller & Colloca, 2009).

Beyond Placebo Pills: The Impact of the Patient-Clinician Relationship

While the use of placebo pills in clinical practice remains controversial, placebo effects are central in daily clinical practice and clinician-doctor relationships (Brody & Miller, 2011). Formal ritualized encounters, notably including a supportive patient-clinician relationship, can indeed trigger placebo effects (Jonas, 2011). For example, irritable bowel syndrome (IBS) patients in a randomized, sham-controlled acupuncture trial assigned to three groups with different patient-clinician interactions (treatment with minimal interaction, with augmented interaction, and wait-list) showed significant relief, primarily in the augmented interaction group (Kaptchuk et al., 2008). Furthermore, patients with post-operative pain and anxiety required substantially lower dose of morphine and benzodiazepines when treatments were delivered by informing patients about the time and benefit of treatments (Amanzio, Pollo, Maggi, & Benedetti, 2001; Colloca et al., 2004). The same treatments delivered by a computerized-pump of infusion were less or not efficacious. This so-called "overt" and "covert" administration of treatment suggests that the placebo effect is part of any treatment and that *enhanced* therapeutic outcomes can be achieved without any placebos (Colloca et al., 2004).

These and other studies suggest that a caring, mutually respectful and engaged relationship with the patient can lead to placebo-mediated benefits (Brody, 1980, 1997).

The ostensibly ordinary encounter between patient and clinician constitutes a pervasive medical ritual (Adler & Hammett, 1973). Research on placebo effects provides a substantial body of neurobiological and psychological evidence underscoring the importance of encouragement of positive expectations, hallmarks of caring clinical interaction (Brody & Miller, 2011). Clearly there is no harm in harnessing placebo effects in medicine, as long as deception is avoided. Accordingly, the study of the placebo effect should be incorporated in the core clinical practice curriculum of all health practitioners. However, whether placebos can or should be otherwise intentionally used is still a subject for ongoing and future research.

Key Messages

- Clinicians should convene to produce guidance on how to address the potential demand for the use of placebos and placebo effects with clear and unequivocal recommendations.
- Clinicians should lay out the rationale and justification to guide decision making as evidence evolves, and a transparent process would be needed for weighing benefits and risks associated with the use of placebos and placebo effects.
- Scientific investigation of placebo effects holds the promise of guiding the art of medicine in service of patient care.
- The study of the placebo effect should be incorporated in the core clinical practice curriculum of all health practitioners.

Acknowledgments

This research was supported by the Intramural Program of the National Center for Complementary and Alternative Medicine, National Institute of Mental Health, the Clinical Center at the National Institutes of Health, and the Samueli Institute.
This work was developed by first convening representatives from academia, not-for-profit organizations, and pharmaceutical industry with expertise in placebo research at the National Institutes of Health. A subgroup of members including Luana Colloca, MD, PhD, Wayne B. Jonas, MD, John Killen, Jr., MD, Franklin G. Miller PhD, and David Shurtleff, PhD, subsequently refined the emerging concepts and drafted the manuscript. The opinions expressed by the authors are those of the authors and do not necessarily reflect the position or policy of the National Institutes of Health, the Public Health Service, or the Department of Health and Human Services.
Conflicts of interest: none.

References

Adler, H. M., & Hammett, V. B. (1973). The doctor-patient relationship revisited. An analysis of the placebo effect. *Annals of Internal Medicine, 78*, 595–598.
Amanzio, M., Pollo, A., Maggi, G., & Benedetti, F. (2001). Response variability to analgesics: A role for non-specific activation of endogenous opioids. *Pain, 90*, 205–215.
Benedetti, F. (2008). Mechanisms of placebo and placebo-related effects across diseases and treatments. *Annual Review of Pharmacology and Toxicology, 48*, 33–60. doi: 10.1146/annurev.pharmtox.48.113006.094711
Bingel, U., Wanigasekera, V., Wiech, K., Ni Mhuircheartaigh, R., Lee, M. C., Ploner, M., & Tracey, I. (2011). The effect of treatment expectation on drug efficacy: Imaging the analgesic benefit of the opioid remifentanil. *Science Translational Medicine, 3*, 70ra14. doi: 10.1126/scitranslmed.3001244
Brody, H. (1980). *Placebo and the philosophy of medicine*. Chicago, IL: University of Chicago Press.
Brody, H. (1997). Placebo response, sustained partnership, and emotional resilience in practice. *American Board of Family Medicine, 10*, 72–74.
Brody, H., & Miller, F. G. (2011). Lessons from recent research about the placebo effect – from art to science. *Journal of the American Medical Association, 306*, 2612–2613. doi: 10.1001/jama.2011.1850
Colloca, L., & Finniss, D. (2012). Nocebo effects, patient-clinician communication, and therapeutic outcomes. *Journal of the American Medical Association, 307*, 567–568. doi: 307/6/567 [pii] 10.1001/jama.2012.115
Colloca, L., Klinger, R., Flor, H., & Bingel, U. (2013). Placebo analgesia: Psychological and neurobiological mechanisms. *Pain, 154*, 511–514. doi: 10.1016/j.pain.2013.02.002
Colloca, L., Lopiano, L., Lanotte, M., & Benedetti, F. (2004). Overt versus covert treatment for pain, anxiety, and Parkinson's disease. *Lancet Neurology, 3*, 679–684. doi: S1474442204009081 [pii] 10.1016/S1474-4422(04)00908-1
Colloca, L., & Miller, F. (2013). Placebo and nocebo: Ethical challenges and solutions. In L. Colloca, M. A. Flaten, & K. Meissner (Eds.), *Placebo and pain: From bench to bedside* (pp. 277–286). Oxford, UK: Elsevier.

Colloca, L., & Miller, F. G. (2011). Harnessing the placebo effect: The need for translational research. *Philosophical Transactions of the Royal Society B: Biological Sciences, 366*, 1922–1930. doi: 10.1098/rstb.2010.0399

Di Blasi, Z., & Reilly, D. (2005). Placebos in medicine: Medical paradoxes need disentangling. *British Medical Journal, 330*, 45. doi: 10.1136/bmj.330.7481.45-a

Enck, P., Bingel, U., Schedlowski, M., & Rief, W. (2013). The placebo response in medicine: Minimize, maximize or personalize? *Nature Reviews Drug Discovery, 12*, 191–204. doi: 10.1038/nrd3923

Fassler, M., Meissner, K., Schneider, A., & Linde, K. (2010). Frequency and circumstances of placebo use in clinical practice – a systematic review of empirical studies. *BMC Medicine, 8*, 15. doi: 10.1186/1741-7015-8-15

Howick, J., Bishop, F. L., Heneghan, C., Wolstenholme, J., Stevens, S., Hobbs, F. D., & Lewith, G. (2013). Placebo use in the United Kingdom: Results from a national survey of primary care practitioners. *PLoS One, 8*, e58247. doi: 10.1371/journal.pone.0058247

Hrobjartsson, A., & Norup, M. (2003). The use of placebo interventions in medical practice – a national questionnaire survey of Danish clinicians. *Evaluation & the Health Professions, 26*, 153–165.

Jonas, W. B. (2011). Reframing placebo in research and practice. *Philosophical Transactions of the Royal Society B: Biological Sciences, 366*, 1896–1904. doi: 10.1098/rstb.2010.0405

Kaptchuk, T. J., Friedlander, E., Kelley, J. M., Sanchez, M. N., Kokkotou, E., Singer, J. P., ... Lembo, A. J. (2010). Placebos without deception: A randomized controlled trial in irritable bowel syndrome. *PLoS One, 5*, e15591. doi: 10.1371/journal.pone.0015591

Kaptchuk, T. J., Kelley, J. M., Conboy, L. A., Davis, R. B., Kerr, C. E., Jacobson, E. E., ... Lembo, A. J. (2008). Components of placebo effect: Randomised controlled trial in patients with irritable bowel syndrome. *British Medical Journal, 336*, 999–1003. doi: 10.1136/bmj.39524.439618.25

Klinger, R., Colloca, L., Bingel, U., & Flor, H. (2014). Placebo analgesia: Clinical applications. *Pain, 155*, 1055–1058. doi: 10.1016/j.pain.2013.12.007

Linde, K., Fassler, M., & Meissner, K. (2011). Placebo interventions, placebo effects and clinical practice. *Philosophical Transactions of the Royal Society B: Biological Sciences, 366*, 1905–1912. doi: 10.1098/rstb.2010.0383

McRae, C., Cherin, E., Yamazaki, T. G., Diem, G., Vo, A. H., Russell, D., ... Freed, C. R. (2004). Effects of perceived treatment on quality of life and medical outcomes in a double-blind placebo surgery trial. *Archives of General Psychiatry, 61*, 412–420. doi: 10.1001/archpsyc.61.4.412

Meissner, K., Bingel, U., Colloca, L., Wager, T. D., Watson, A., & Flaten, M. A. (2011). The placebo effect: Advances from different methodological approaches. *Journal of Neuroscience, 31*, 16117–16124. doi: 10.1523/JNEUROSCI.4099-11.2011

Meissner, K., Hofner, L., Fassler, M., & Linde, K. (2012). Widespread use of pure and impure placebo interventions by GPs in Germany. *Family Practice, 29*, 79–85. doi: 10.1093/fampra/cmr045

Miller, F. G., & Colloca, L. (2009). The legitimacy of placebo treatments in clinical practice: Evidence and ethics. *American Journal of Bioethics, 9*, 39–47. doi: 10.1080/15265160903316263

Tilburt, J. C., Emanuel, E. J., Kaptchuk, T. J., Curlin, F. A., & Miller, F. G. (2008). Prescribing "placebo treatments": Results of national survey of US internists and rheumatologists. *British Medical Journal, 337*, a1938. doi: 10.1136/bmj.a1938

Wechsler, M. E., Kelley, J. M., Boyd, I. O., Dutile, S., Marigowda, G., Kirsch, I., ... Kaptchuk, T. J. (2011). Active albuterol or placebo, sham acupuncture, or no intervention in asthma. *New England Journal of Medicine, 365*, 119–126. doi: 10.1056/NEJMoa1103319

Luana Colloca

National Institutes of Health
Clinical Center
10 Center Drive, 10/1C154
Bethesda, MD 20892-1156
USA
Tel. +1 301 435-8715
Fax +1 301 496-0760
E-mail luana.colloca@nih.gov

Review Article

Antidepressants and the Placebo Effect

Irving Kirsch

Harvard Medical School, Beth Israel Deaconess Medical Center, Boston, MA, USA

Abstract. Antidepressants are supposed to work by fixing a chemical imbalance, specifically, a lack of serotonin in the brain. Indeed, their supposed effectiveness is the primary evidence for the chemical imbalance theory. But analyses of the published data and the unpublished data that were hidden by drug companies reveals that most (if not all) of the benefits are due to the placebo effect. Some antidepressants increase serotonin levels, some decrease it, and some have no effect at all on serotonin. Nevertheless, they all show the same therapeutic benefit. Even the small statistical difference between antidepressants and placebos may be an enhanced placebo effect, due to the fact that most patients and doctors in clinical trials successfully break blind. The serotonin theory is as close as any theory in the history of science to having been proved wrong. Instead of curing depression, popular antidepressants may induce a biological vulnerability making people more likely to become depressed in the future.

Keywords: depression, antidepressants, effectiveness, serotonin, placebo

On February 26, 2008, an article about antidepressants that my colleagues and I wrote was published in the journal PLoS Medicine (Kirsch et al., 2008). That morning, I awoke to find that our paper was the front page story in all of the leading national newspapers in the United Kingdom. A few months later, Random House invited me to expand the article into a book, entitled *The Emperor's New Drugs: Exploding the Antidepressant Myth*, which has since been translated into French, Italian, Japanese, Polish, and Turkish (Kirsch, 2009). Two years later, the book, and the research reported in it, was the topic of a five-page cover story in the influential American news magazine, *Newsweek*. And 2 years after that, it was the focus of a 15-min segment on *60 Minutes*, America's top-rated television news program. Somehow, I had been transformed, from a mild-mannered university professor into a media superhero – or super villain, depending on whom you asked. What had my colleagues and I done do warrant this transformation?

To answer that question, we have to go back to 1998, when a former graduate student, Guy Sapirstein, and I published a meta-analysis on antidepressants in an online journal of the American Psychological Association (Kirsch & Sapirstein, 1998). When they were new, meta-analyses were somewhat controversial and our article was accompanied by an editorial warning to that effect – not unlike the suicide warning that the US Food and Drug Administration (FDA) requires for antidepressants. But now meta-analyses are published in all of the major medical journals, where they are widely considered to be the best and most reliable way of making sense of the data from studies with different and sometimes conflicting results.

When Sapirstein and I began our analysis of the antidepressant clinical trial data, we were not particularly interested in antidepressants. Instead, we were interested in understanding the placebo effect. I have been fascinated by the placebo effect for my entire academic career. How is it, I wondered, that the belief that one has taken a medication can produce some of the effects of that medication?

It seemed to Sapirstein and me that depression was a good place to look for placebo effects. After all, one of the prime characteristics of depression is the sense of hopelessness that depressed people feel. If you ask depressed people to tell you what the worst thing in their life is, many will tell you that it is their depression. The British psychologist John Teasdale called this being depressed about depression (Teasdale, 1985). If that is the case, then the mere promise of an effective treatment should help to alleviate depression, by replacing hopelessness with hopefulness – the hope that one will recover after all. It was with this in mind that we set out to measure the placebo effect in depression.

We searched the literature for studies in which depressed patients had been randomized to receive an inert placebo or no treatment at all. The studies we found also included data on the response to antidepressants, because that was the only place one finds data on the response to placebo among depressed patients. I was not particularly interested in the drug effect. I assumed that antidepressants were effective. As a psychotherapist, I sometimes referred my severely depressed clients for prescriptions of antidepressant drugs. Sometimes the condition of my clients improved when they began taking antidepressants; sometimes it did not. When it did, I assumed it was the effect of the drug that was making them better. Given my long standing interest in the placebo effect, I should have known better, but back then I did not.

Analyzing the data we had found, we were not surprised to find a substantial placebo effect on depression. What surprised us was how small the drug effect was. Seventy-five percent of the improvement in the drug group also occurred when people were give dummy pills with no active ingredient in them. Needless to say, our meta-analysis proved to be very controversial. Its publication led to heated exchanges (e.g., Beutler, 1998; Kirsch, 1998; Klein, 1998). The response from critics was that these data could not be accurate. Perhaps our search had led us to analyze an unrepresentative subset of clinical trials. Antidepressants had been evaluated in many trials, the critics said, and their effectiveness had been well established.

In an effort to response to these critics, we decided to replicate our study with a different set of clinical trials (Kirsch, Moore, Scoboria, & Nicholls, 2002). To do this, we used the Freedom of Information Act to request that the Food and Drug Administration (FDA) send us the data that pharmaceutical companies had sent to it in the process of obtaining approval for six new generation antidepressants that accounted for the bulk of antidepressant prescriptions being written at the time. There are a number of advantages to the FDA data set. Most important, the FDA requires that the pharmaceutical companies provide information on all of the clinical trials that they have sponsored. Thus, we had data on unpublished trials as well as published trials. This turned out to be very important. Almost half of the clinical trials sponsored by the drug companies have not been published (Melander, Ahlqvist-Rastad, Meijer, & Beermann, 2003; Turner, Matthews, Linardatos, Tell, & Rosenthal, 2008). The results of the unpublished trials were known only to the drug companies and the FDA, and most of them failed to find a significant benefit of drug over placebo. A second advantage of the FDA trials in the FDA dataset is that they all used the same primary measure of depression – the Hamilton depression scale (HAM-D). That made it easy to understand the clinical significance of the drug-placebo differences. Finally, the data in the FDA files were the basis upon which the medications were approved. In that sense they have a privileged status. If there is anything wrong with those trials, the medications should not have been approved in the first place.

In the data sent to us by the FDA, only 43% of the trials showed a statistically significant benefit of drug over placebo. The remaining 57% were failed or negative trials. Similar results have been reported in other meta-analyses (Turner et al., 2008), including one conducted by the FDA on the clinical trials of all antidepressants that it had approved between 1983 and 2008 (Khin, Chen, Yang, Yang, & Laughren, 2011). The results of our analysis indicated that the placebo response was 82% of the response to these antidepressants. Subsequently, my colleagues and I replicated our meta-analysis on a larger number of trials that had been submitted to the FDA (Kirsch et al., 2008). With this expanded data set, we found once again that 82% of the drug response was duplicated by placebo. More important, in both analyses, the mean difference between drug and placebo was less than two points on the HAM-D. The HAM-D is a 17-item scale on which people can score from 0 to 53 points, depending on how depressed they are. A six-point difference can be obtained just by changes in sleep patterns, with no change in any other symptom of depression. So the 1.8 difference that we found between drug and placebo was very small indeed – small enough to be clinically insignificant. But you don't have to take my word for how small this difference is. The National Institute for Health and Care Excellence (NICE), which drafts treatment guidelines for the National Health Service in the United Kingdom, has established a three-point difference between drug and placebo on the HAM-D as a criterion of clinical significance (NICE, 2004). Thus, when published and unpublished data are combined, they fail to show a clinically significant advantage for antidepressant medication over inert placebo.

I should mention here the difference between *statistical* significance and *clinical* significance. Statistical significance concerns how reliable an effect is. Is it a real effect, or is it just due to chance? Statistical significance does not tell you anything about the size of the effect. Clinical significance, on the other hand, deals with the size of an effect and whether it would make any difference in a person's life. Imagine, for example, that a study of 500,000 people has shown that smiling increases life expectancy – by 5 min. With 500,000 subjects, I can virtually guarantee you that this difference will be statistically significant, but it is clinically meaningless.

The results of our analyses have since been replicated repeatedly (Fountoulakis & Möller, 2011; Fournier et al., 2010; NICE, 2004; Turner et al., 2008). Some of the replications used our data; others analyzed different sets of clinical trials. The FDA even did its own meta-analysis on all of the antidepressants that they have approved (Khin et al., 2011). But and despite differences in the way the data have been spun, the numbers are remarkably consistent. Differences on the HAM-D are small – always below the criterion set by NICE. Thomas P. Laughren, the director of the FDA's psychiatry products division, acknowledged this on the American television news program *60 Minutes*. He said, "I think we all agree that the changes that you see in the short-term trials, the difference in improvement between drug and placebo is rather small."

And it is not only the short-term trials that show a small, clinically insignificant difference between drug and placebo. In their meta-analysis of published clinical trials, NICE (2004) found that the difference between drug and placebo in the long-term trials were no larger than those in short-term trials.

Severity of Depression and Antidepressant Effectiveness

Critics of our 2002 meta-analysis argued that our results were based on clinical trials conducted on subjects who were not very depressed (e.g., Hollon, DeRubeis, Shelton,

& Weiss, 2002; Thase, 2002). In more depressed patients, they argued, a more substantial difference might be found. This criticism led my colleagues and I to reanalyze the FDA data in 2008 (Kirsch et al., 2008). We categorized the clinical trials in the FDA database according to the severity of the patients' depression at the beginning of the trial, using conventionally used categories of depression. As it turns out, all but one of the trials were conducted on moderately depressed patients, and that trial failed to show any significant difference between drug and placebo. Indeed, the difference was virtually nil (0.07 points on the HAM-D). All of the rest of the trials were conducted on patients whose mean baseline scores put them in the "very severe" category of depression, and even among these patients, the drug-placebo difference was below the level of clinical significance.

Still, severity did make a difference. Patients at the very extreme end of depression severity, those scoring at least 28 on the HAM-D, showed an average drug-placebo difference of 4.36 points. To find out how many patients fell within this extremely depressed group, I asked Mark Zimmerman from the Brown University School of Medicine to send me the raw data from a study in which he and his colleagues assessed HAM-D scores of patients who had been diagnosed with unipolar major depressive disorder (MDD) after presenting for an intake at a psychiatric outpatient practice (Zimmerman, Chelminski, & Posternak, 2005). Patients with HAM-D scores of 28 or above represented 11% of these patients. This suggests that 89% of depressed patients are not receiving a clinically significant benefit from the antidepressants that are prescribed for them.

Yet this 11% figure may overestimate the number of people who benefit from antidepressants. Antidepressants are also prescribed to people who do not qualify for the diagnosis of major depression. My neighbor's pet dog died; his physician prescribed an antidepressant. A friend in the US was diagnosed with lumbar muscle spasms and was prescribed an antidepressant. I have lost count of the number of people who have told me they were prescribed antidepressants when complaining of insomnia – even though insomnia is a frequently reported side effect of antidepressants. About 20% of patients suffering from insomnia in the United States are given antidepressants as a treatment by their primary care physicians (Simon & VonKorff, 1997), despite the fact that "the popularity of antidepressants in the treatment of insomnia is not supported by a large amount of convincing data, but rather by opinions and beliefs of the prescribing physicians" (Wiegand, 2008, p. 2411).

Predicting Response to Treatment

Severity of depression is one of the few predictors of response to treatment. Type of antidepressant little if any impact on treatment response. As summarized in a 2011 meta-analysis of studies comparing one antidepressant to another:

> On the basis of 234 studies, no clinically relevant differences in efficacy or effectiveness were detected for the treatment of acute, continuation, and maintenance phases of MDD. No differences in efficacy were seen in patients with accompanying symptoms or in subgroups based on age, sex, ethnicity, or comorbid conditions... Current evidence does not warrant recommending a particular second-generation antidepressant on the basis of differences in efficacy (Gartlehner et al., 2011, p. 772).

Although type of medication does not make a clinically significant difference in outcome, response to placebo does. Almost all antidepressant trials include a placebo run-in phase. Before the trial begins, all of the patients are given a placebo for a week or two. After this run-in period, the patients are reassessed, and anyone who has improved substantially is excluded from the trial. That leaves patients who have not benefitted at all from placebo and those who have benefited only a little bit. These are the patients who are randomized to be given drug or kept on placebo. As it turns out, the patients who show at least a little improvement during the run-in period are the ones most likely to respond to the real drug, as shown not only by physician ratings, but also by changes in brain function (Hunter, Leuchter, Morgan, & Cook, 2006; Quitkin et al., 1998).

How Did These Drugs Get Approved?

How is it possible that medications with such weak efficacy data were approved by the FDA? The answer lies in an understanding of the approval criteria used by the FDA. The FDA requires two adequately conducted clinical trials showing a significant difference between drug and placebo. But there is a loophole: There is no limit to the number of trials that can be conducted in search of these two significant trials. Trials showing negative results simply do not count. Furthermore, the clinical significance of the findings is not considered. All that matters is that the results are statistically significant.

The most egregious example of the implementation of this criterion is provided by the FDA's approval of vilazodone in 2011. Seven controlled efficacy trials were conducted. The first five failed to show any significant differences on any measure of depression, and the mean drug-placebo difference in these studies was less than ½ point on the HAM-D, and in two of the three trials, the direction of the difference actually favored the placebo. The company ran two more studies and managed to obtain small but significant drug-placebo differences (1.70 points). The mean drug-placebo difference across the seven studies was 1.01 HAM-D points. This was sufficient for the FDA to grant approval, and the information approved by the FDA for informing doctors and patients reads, "The efficacy of VIIBRYD was established in two 8-week, randomized, double-blind, placebo-controlled trials." No mention is made of the five failed trials that preceded the two successful ones.

The failure to mention the unsuccessful trials was not merely an oversight; it reflects a carefully decided FDA policy dating back for decades. To my knowledge, there is only one antidepressant in which the FDA included information on the existence of negative trials. The exception is citalopram, and the inclusion of the information followed an objection raised by Paul Leber, who was at the time the director of the FDA Division of Neuropharmacological Drug Products. In an internal memo dated May 4, 1998, Leber wrote:

> One aspect of the labeling deserves special mention. The [report] not only describes the clinical trials providing evidence of citalopram's antidepressant effects, but make mention of adequate and well-controlled clinical studies that failed to do so... The Office Director is inclined toward the view that the provision of such information is of no practical value to either the patient or prescriber. I disagree. I believe it is useful for the prescriber, patient, and 3rd-party payer to know, without having to gain access to official FDA review documents, that citalopram's antidepressants effects were not detected in every controlled clinical trial intended to demonstrate those effects. I am aware that clinical studies often fail to document the efficacy of effective drugs, but I doubt that the public, or even the majority of the medical community, is aware of this fact. I am persuaded that they not only have a right to know but that they should know. Moreover, I believe that labeling that selectively describes positive studies and excludes mention of negative ones can be viewed as potentially "false and misleading." (Leber, May 4, 1998).

Hooray for Paul Leber. I have never met or corresponded with this gentleman, but because of this courageous memo, he is one of my heroes.

The Serotonin Myth

Over the years, I have noticed something very strange in the antidepressant literature. When different antidepressants are compared with each other, their effects are remarkable similar. I first noticed this when Guy Sapirstein did our 1998 meta-analysis of the published literature. When we first saw how small the actual drug effect was, we thought we might have done something wrong. Perhaps we had erred by including trials that had evaluated different types of antidepressants. Maybe we are underestimating the true effectiveness of antidepressants by including clinical trials of drugs that were less effective than others.

Before submitting our paper for publication, we went back to the data and examined the type of antidepressant used each trial. Some were selective serotonin reuptake inhibitors (SSRIs), others were tricyclic medications, we lumped together the trials on antidepressant drugs that were neither SSRIs nor tricyclics and called them "other antidepressants." And then we noticed that there was a fourth category of drugs in the trials were had analyzed. These were trials in which drugs that are not thought to be antidepressants at all – tranquilizers and thyroid medications, for example – were given to depressed patients and evaluated for their effect on depression.

When we analyzed the drug and placebo response for each type of drug, we found another surprise awaiting us. It did not matter what kind of drug the patients had been given in the trial. The response to the drug was always the same, and 75% of that response was also found in the placebo groups. I recall being impressed by how unusual the similarity in results was, but I have since learned that they are not unusual at all. I have since encountered this phenomenon over and over again. In the STAR*D trial, which, at a cost of $35,000,000, is the most costly clinical trial of antidepressants ever conducted, patients who did not respond to the prescribed SSRI were switched to a different antidepressant (Rush et al., 2006). Some were switched to a SNRI (serotonin-noradrenalin-reuptake-inhibitor), a drug that is supposed to increase norepinephrine as well as of serotonin in the brain. Others were switched to an NDRI (norepinephrine-dopamine reuptake inhibitor), which is supposed to increase norepinephrine and dopamine, without affecting serotonin at all. And still others were simply given a different SSRI. About one out of four patients responded clinically to the new drug, but it did not matter which new drug they were given. The effects ranged from 26% to 28%; in other words, they were exactly the same regardless of type of drug.

The most commonly prescribed antidepressants are SSRIs, drugs that are supposed to selectively target the neurotransmitter serotonin. But there is another antidepressant that has a very different mode of action. It is called tianeptine, and it has been approved for prescription as an antidepressant by the French drug regulatory agency. Tianeptine is an SSRE, a selective serotonin reuptake enhancer. Instead of increasing the amount of serotonin in the brain, it is supposed to decrease it. If the theory that depression is caused by a deficiency of serotonin were correct, we would expect to make depression worse. But it doesn't. In clinical trials comparing the effects of tianeptine to those of SSRIs and tricyclic antidepressants, 63% of patients show significant improvement (defined as a 50% reduction in symptoms), the same response rate that is found for SSRIs, NDRIs, and tricyclics, in this type of trial (Wagstaff, Ormrod, & Spencer, 2001). It simply does not matter what is in the medication – it might increase serotonin, decrease it, or have no effect on serotonin at all. The effect on depression is the same.

What do you call pills, the effects of which are independent of their chemical composition? I call them "placebos."

Antidepressants as Active Placebos

All antidepressants seem to be equally effective, and although the difference between drug and placebo is not clinically significant, it is significant statistically. This leads to the obvious question: What do all of these active drugs have in common that make their effect on depression slightly, but statistically significantly, better than placebo?

One think that antidepressants have in common is that they all produce side effects. Why is that important? Imagine that you are a subject in a clinical trial. You are told that the trial is double blind and that you might be given a placebo. You are told what the side effects of the medication are. The therapeutic effects of the drug may take weeks to notice, but the side effects might occur more quickly. Would you not wonder to which group you had been assigned, drug or placebo? And noticing one of the listed side effects, would you not conclude that you had been given the real drug? In one study, 89% of the patients in the drug group correctly "guessed" that they had been given the real antidepressant, a result that is very unlikely to be due to chance (Rabkin et al., 1986).

In other words, clinical trials are not really double blind. Many patients in clinical trials realize that they have been given the real drug, rather than the placebo, most likely because of the drug's side effects. What effect is this likely to have in a clinical trial? We do not have to guess at the answer to this question. Bret Rutherford and his colleagues at Columbia University have provided the answer. They examined the response to antidepressants in studies that did not have a placebo group with those in studies where they did have a placebo group (Rutherford, Sneed, & Roose, 2009). The main difference between these studies is that in the first case, the patients were certain they were getting an active antidepressant, where as in the placebo-controlled trials, they knew that they might be given a placebo. Knowing for sure that they were getting an active drug boosted the effectiveness of the drug significantly. This supports the hypothesis that the relatively small difference between drug and placebo in antidepressant trials are at least in part due to "breaking blind" and discerning that one is in the drug group, because of the side effects produced by the drug.

What to Do?

To summarize, there is a strong therapeutic response to antidepressant medication. But the response to placebo is almost as strong. This presents a therapeutic dilemma. The drug effect of antidepressants is not clinically significant, but the placebo effect is. What should be done clinically in light of these findings?

One possibility would be to use antidepressants as active placebos. But the risks involved in antidepressant use render this alternative problematic (Andrews, Thomson, Amstadter, & Neale, 2012; Domar, Moragianni, Ryley, & Urato, 2013; Serretti & Chiesa, 2009). Among the side effects of antidepressants are sexual dysfunction (which affects 70–80% of patients on SSRIs), long-term weight gain, insomnia, nausea, and diarrhea. Approximately 20% of people attempted to quit taking antidepressants show withdrawal symptoms. Antidepressants have been linked to increases in suicidal ideation among children and young adults. Older adults have increased risks of stroke and death from all causes. Pregnant women using antidepressants are at increased risk of miscarriage, and if they don't miscarry, their offspring are more likely to be born with autism, birth malformations, persistent pulmonary hypertension, and newborn behavioral syndrome. Furthermore, some of these risks have been linked to antidepressant use during the first trimester of pregnancy, when women may not be aware that they are pregnant. Perhaps the most surprising health consequence of antidepressant use is one that affects people of all ages. Antidepressants increase the risk of relapse after one has recovered. People are more likely to become depressed again after treatment by antidepressants than after treatment by other means – including placebo treatment (Andrews et al., 2012; Babyak et al., 2000; Dobson et al., 2008). Furthermore, the degree to which the risk of relapse increases depends on the degree to which the particular antidepressant used changes neurotransmission in the brain. Given these health risks, antidepressants should not be used as a first-line treatment for depression.

Another possibility is to prescribe placebos. They are almost as effective as antidepressants, but elicit far fewer side effects. Surveys indicated that many physicians do in fact prescribe placebos (Raz et al., 2011; Tilburt, Emanuel, Kaptchuk, Curlin, & Miller, 2008). The conventional wisdom is that for a placebo to be effective, patients must believe they are receiving active medication, which entails deception. Besides being ethically questionable, the practice of deceiving patients runs the risk of undermining trust, which may be one of the most important clinical tools that clinicians have at their disposal. But is the conventional wisdom correct? My colleagues and I have tested and confirmed the hypothesis that placebos can be effective even when given openly, without deception, when given in the context of a warm therapeutic relationship and with an honest but convincing rationale as to why they should be effective (Kaptchuk et al., 2010). Our study targeted irritable bowel syndrome, rather than depression, but a small pilot study suggests that it might also work in the treatment of depression (Kelley, Kaptchuk, Cusin, Lipkin, & Fava, 2012). Until this is confirmed, however, placebo treatment is not a viable option.

Fortunately, placebos are not the only alternative to antidepressant treatment. My colleagues and I have conducted a meta-analysis of various treatments for depression, including antidepressants, psychotherapy, the combination of psychotherapy and antidepressants, and "alternative" treatments, which included acupuncture and physical exercise (Khan, Faucett, Lichtenberg, Kirsch, & Brown, 2012). We found no significant differences between these treatments or within different types of psychotherapy. When different treatments are equally effective, choice should be based on risk and harm, and of all of these treatments, antidepressant drugs are the riskiest and most harmful. If they are to be used at all, it should be as a last resort, when depression is extremely severe and all other treatment alternatives have been tried and failed.

References

Andrews, P. W., Thomson, J. A., Amstadter, A., & Neale, M. C. (2012). Primum non nocere: An evolutionary analysis of whether antidepressants do more harm than good. [Review]. *Frontiers in Psychology, 3*, 117. doi: 10.3389/fpsyg.2012.00117

Babyak, M. A., Blumenthal, J. A., Herman, S., Khatri, P., Doraiswamy, P. M., Moore, K. A., ... Krishnan, K. R. (2000). Exercise treatment for major depression: Maintenance of therapeutic benefit at 10 months. *Psychosomatic Medicine, 62*, 633–638.

Beutler, L. E. (1998). Prozac and placebo: There's a pony in there somewhere. *Prevention & Treatment, 1*, 3c. doi: 10.1037/1522-3736.1.2.13c

Dobson, K. S., Hollon, S. D., Dimidjian, S., Schmaling, K. B., Kohlenberg, R. J., Gallop, R. J., ... Jacobson, N. S. (2008). Randomized trial of behavioral activation, cognitive therapy, and antidepressant medication in the prevention of relapse and recurrence in major depression. *Journal of Consulting and Clinical Psychology, 76*, 468–477. doi: 10.1037/0022-006X.76.3.468

Domar, A. D., Moragianni, V. A., Ryley, D. A., & Urato, A. C. (2013). The risks of selective serotonin reuptake inhibitor use in infertile women: A review of the impact on fertility, pregnancy, neonatal health and beyond. *Human Reproduction, 28*, 160–171. doi: 10.1093/humrep/des383

Fountoulakis, K. N., & Möller, H. J. (2011). Efficacy of antidepressants: A re-analysis and re-interpretation of the Kirsch data. *International Journal of Neuro-Psychopharmacology, 14*, 405.

Fournier, J. C., DeRubeis, R. J., Hollon, S. D., Dimidjian, S., Amsterdam, J. D., Shelton, R. C., & Fawcett, J. (2010). Antidepressant drug effects and depression severity: a patient-level meta-analysis. *Journal of the American Medical Association, 303*, 47–53. doi: 10.1001/jama.2009.1943

Gartlehner, G., Hansen, R. A., Morgan, L. C., Thaler, K., Lux, L., Van Noord, M., ... Lohr, K. N. (2011). Comparative benefits and harms of second-generation antidepressants for treating major depressive disorder. *Annals of Internal Medicine, 155*, 772–785. doi: 10.1059/0003-4819-155-11-201112060-00009

Hollon, S. D., DeRubeis, R. J., Shelton, R. C., & Weiss, B. (2002). The emperor's new drugs: Effect size and moderation effects. *Prevention and Treatment, 5*, 28. doi: 10.1037/1522-3736.5.1.528c

Hunter, A. M., Leuchter, A. F., Morgan, M. L., & Cook, I. A. (2006). Changes in brain function (quantitative eeg cordance) during placebo lead-in and treatment outcomes in clinical trials for major depression. *American Journal of Psychiatry, 163*, 1426–1432.

Kaptchuk, T. J., Friedlander, E., Kelley, J. M., Sanchez, M. N., Kokkotou, E., Singer, J. P., ... Lembo, A. J. (2010). Placebos without deception: A randomized controlled trial in irritable bowel syndrome. *PLoS One, 5*, e15591. doi: 10.1371/journal.pone.0015591

Kelley, J. M., Kaptchuk, T. J., Cusin, C., Lipkin, S., & Fava, M. (2012). Open-label placebo for major depressive disorder: A pilot randomized controlled trial. *Psychotherapy and Psychosomatics, 81*, 312–314.

Khan, A., Faucett, J., Lichtenberg, P., Kirsch, I., & Brown, W. A. (2012). A systematic review of comparative efficacy of treatments and controls for depression. *PLoS One, 7*, e41778. doi: 10.1371/journal.pone.0041778

Khin, N. A., Chen, Y. F., Yang, Y., Yang, P., & Laughren, T. P. (2011). Exploratory analyses of efficacy data from major depressive disorder trials submitted to the US Food and Drug Administration in support of new drug applications. *Journal of Clinical Psychiatry, 72*, 464–472. doi: 10.4088/JCP.10m06191

Kirsch, I. (1998). Reducing noise and hearing placebo more clearly. *Prevention & Treatment, 1*, 7r. doi: 10.1037/1522-3736.1.1.17r

Kirsch, I. (2009). *The emperor's new drugs: Exploding the antidepressant myth*. London, UK: Bodley Head.

Kirsch, I., Deacon, B. J., Huedo-Medina, T. B., Scoboria, A., Moore, T. J., & Johnson, B. T. (2008). Initial severity and antidepressant benefits: A meta-analysis of data submitted to the Food and Drug Administration. *PLoS Medicine, 5*, e45. doi: 10.1371/journal.pmed.0050045

Kirsch, I., Moore, T. J., Scoboria, A., & Nicholls, S. S. (2002). The emperor's new drugs: An analysis of antidepressant medication data submitted to the U.S. Food and Drug Administration. *Prevention and Treatment, 5*, 23. doi: 10.1037/1522-3736.5.1.523a

Kirsch, I., & Sapirstein, G. (1998). Listening to Prozac but hearing placebo: A meta-analysis of antidepressant medication. *Prevention and Treatment, 1*, 2a. doi: 10.1037/1522-3736.1.1.12a

Klein, D. F. (1998). Listening to meta-analysis but hearing bias. *Prevention & Treatment, 1*, 6c. doi: 10.1037/1522-3736.1.1.16c

Leber, P. (1998). Approvable action on Forrest Laboratories, Inc. NDA 20-822 Celexa (citalopram HBr) for the management of depression. In *Memoradum to the Department of Health and Human Services, Public Health Service, Food and Drug Administration, Center for Drug Evaluation and Research* May 4. Washington, DC: FDA.

Melander, H., Ahlqvist-Rastad, J., Meijer, G., & Beermann, B. (2003). Evidence b(i)ased medicine – selective reporting from studies sponsored by pharmaceutical industry: Review of studies in new drug applications. *British Medical Journal, 326*, 1171–1173.

NICE. (2004). Depression: Management of depression in primary and secondary care [Clinical practice guideline 23] Retrieved from www.nice.org.uk/page.aspx?o = 235213. London, UK: National Institute for Health and Care Excellence.

Quitkin, F. M., McGrath, P. J., Stewart, J. W., Ocepek-Welikson, K., Taylor, B. P., Nunes, E., ... Klein, D. F. (1998). Placebo run-in period in studies of depressive disorders: Clinical, heuristic and research implications. *British Journal of Psychiatry, 173*, 242–248.

Rabkin, J. G., Markowitz, J. S., Stewart, J. W., McGrath, P. J., Harrison, W., Quitkin, F. M., & Klein, D. F. (1986). How blind is blind? Assessment of patient and doctor medication guesses in a placebo-controlled trial of imipramine and phenelzine. *Psychiatry Research, 19*, 75–86.

Raz, A., Campbell, N., Guindi, D., Holcroft, C., Déry, C., & Cukier, O. (2011). Placebos in clinical practice: A Pan-Canadian Review of attitudes and patterns of use between academic psychiatrists and non-psychiatrists. *Canadian Journal of Psychiatry, 56*, 198–208.

Rush, A. J., Trivedi, M. H., Wisniewski, S. R., Nierenberg, A. A., Stewart, J. W., Warden, D., ... Fava, M. (2006). Acute and longer-term outcomes in depressed outpatients requiring one or several treatment steps: A STAR*D report. *American Journal of Psychiatry, 163*, 1905–1917.

Rutherford, B. R., Sneed, J. R., & Roose, S. P. (2009). Does study design influence outcome? *Psychotherapy and Psychosomatics, 78*, 172–181.

Serretti, A., & Chiesa, A. (2009). Treatment-emergent sexual dysfunction related to antidepressants: A meta-analysis. *Journal of Clinical Psychopharmacology, 29*, 259–266.

Simon, G. E., & VonKorff, M. (1997). Prevalence, burden, and treatment of insomnia in primary care. *American Journal of Psychiatry, 154*, 1417–1423.

Teasdale, J. D. (1985). Psychological treatments for depression: How do they work? *Behaviour Research and Therapy, 23*, 157–165.

Thase, M. E. (2002). Antidepressant effects: The suit may be small, but the fabric is real. *Prevention & Treatment, 5*, 32. doi: 10.1037/1522-3736.5.1.532c

Tilburt, J. C., Emanuel, E. J., Kaptchuk, T. J., Curlin, F. A., & Miller, F. G. (2008). Prescribing "placebo treatments": Results of national survey of US internists and rheumatologists. *British Medical Journal, 337*, 1097–1100. doi: 10.1136/bmj.a1938

Turner, E. H., Matthews, A. M., Linardatos, E., Tell, R. A., & Rosenthal, R. (2008). Selective publication of antidepressant trials and its influence on apparent efficacy. *New England Journal of Medicine, 358*, 252–260.

Wagstaff, A. J., Ormrod, D., & Spencer, C. M. (2001). Tianeptine: A review of its use in depressive disorders. *CNS Drugs, 15*, 231–259.

Wiegand, M. H. (2008). Antidepressants for the treatment of insomnia: A suitable approach? *Drugs, 68*, 2411–2417.

Zimmerman, M., Chelminski, I., & Posternak, M. A. (2005). Generalizability of antidepressant efficacy trials: Differences between depressed psychiatric outpatients who would or would not qualify for an efficacy trial. *American Journal of Psychiatry, 162*, 1370–1372. doi: 10.1176/appi.ajp.162.7.1370

Irving Kirsch

Beth Israel Deaconess Medical Center
Gen. Med. Pricare
330 Brookline Avenue
Boston, MA 02215
USA
Tel. +1 617 945-7827
Fax +1 617 492-3182
E-mail ikirsch@bidmc.harvard.edu

Review Article

Placebo and Nocebo Effects in Chronic Pain Patients

How Expectations and Emotional Feelings Contribute to the Experience of Pain

Lene Vase,[1,2] Ina Skyt,[1,2] Gitte Laue Petersen,[1,2] and Donald D. Price[3]

[1]Department of Psychology and Behavioral Sciences, School of Business and Social Sciences, Aarhus University, Aarhus, Denmark, [2]Danish Pain Research Center, Aarhus University Hospital, Aarhus, Denmark, [3]Division of Neuroscience, Department of Oral and Maxillofacial Surgery, University of Florida, Gainesville, FL, USA

Abstract. Placebo, as well as nocebo, effects have been primarily investigated in studies with healthy volunteers exposed to acute experimental pain. Yet with regard to chronic pain patients, there is emerging evidence for significant placebo effects but not for nocebo effects. Expectations of pain relief are known to contribute to placebo effects, and lately the influence of emotional feelings has also been investigated. In this line of research, an experiential method has been applied to capture the emotional feelings that chronic pain patients experience during placebo and nocebo interventions. The findings indicate that the patients' expectations of treatment effects are highly embedded in their emotional feelings. Hence, in order to optimize placebo factors in the clinical treatment of patients, it may be pivotal to investigate and enhance both expectancies and emotional feelings about treatments.

Keywords: emotional feelings, placebo effects, nocebo effects, chronic pain, experiential method

Our present knowledge of placebo and nocebo effects primarily derives from studies of healthy volunteers exposed to acute experimental pain (Benedetti, 2009; Colloca, Flaten, & Meissner, 2013). Recently, however, significant placebo effects but not nocebo effects have been demonstrated in chronic pain conditions (Kaptchuk et al., 2008, 2010; Klinger, Soost, Flor, & Worm, 2007; Petersen et al., 2012; Price, Craggs, Verne, Perlstein, & Robinson, 2007; Vase, Robinson, Verne, & Price, 2003, 2005; Verne, Robinson, Vase, & Price, 2003). The majority of studies on chronic pain have been conducted with irritable bowel syndrome (IBS) patients where the underlying pathophysiology remains unclear (Piche, Bouin, Arsenault, Poitras, & Rainville, 2011), but large placebo effects have recently also been demonstrated in neuropathic pain where the nerve injury is known (Petersen et al., 2012).

Chronic pain differs from acute and experimental pain in a number of ways. First, chronic pain conditions such as IBS and neuropathic pain are often characterized by a combination of hyperalgesia (increased pain sensitivity) and allodynia (lowered threshold for pain) (Price, 1999; Price & Vase, 2013), indicating that the pain processing in chronic pain patients is different from that of healthy volunteers (Jensen, Dahl, & Arendt-Nielsen, 2013). Second, since chronic pain is ongoing or recurrent, the psychological components of pain processing, including negative expectations, anxiety, and depression, are more pronounced in chronic pain patients (Jensen et al., 2013; Price, 1999).

Psychological processes are likely to influence the patients' experience of pain relief in placebo effects and their experience of pain increase in nocebo effects (Flaten, Aslaksen, & Lyby, 2013; Price & Barrell, 2012; Price, Finniss, & Benedetti, 2008). In order to fully understand the mechanisms underlying placebo and nocebo effects in chronic pain patients, it may be relevant to directly study the contribution of specific cognitions and emotional feelings to the pain-relieving and pain-increasing effects. This may provide the knowledge of how to optimally investigate and enhance these factors in clinical practice (Price & Barrell, 2012; Vase, Norskov, Petersen, & Price, 2011).

In this paper we first outline the magnitude of placebo analgesia and nocebo hyperalgesia effects and review how central psychological factors, such as expectations and emotional feelings, contribute to placebo, and nocebo effects in chronic pain patients. A special focus will be given to the ways of assessing expectations and emotional feelings, and for this purpose we propose the experiential method to investigate patients' direct experiences and emotional feelings during placebo and nocebo interventions. Then we touch upon the clinical implications of the findings.

The Magnitude of Placebo and Nocebo Effects

To understand how expectations and emotional feelings may contribute to placebo and nocebo effects it is helpful to briefly outline the conceptualization and the magnitude of these phenomena. An inactive placebo treatment is typically administered along with verbal suggestions of clinical improvement, thereby making the patients expect pain relief. In the same manner a nocebo treatment is typically given along with verbal suggestions of symptom worsening. The patients expect to feel either better or worse, and eventually do so (Benedetti, 2009; Colloca et al., 2013). In order to differentiate placebo and nocebo effects from spontaneous remission and other confounding factors, they are calculated as the symptom difference between a placebo-treated/nocebo-treated group or condition and a no-treatment group or condition (Benedetti, 2009; Fields & Price, 1997; Price et al., 2008; Vase, Price, Verne, & Robinson, 2004; Vase, Riley, & Price, 2002).

Several meta-analyses have shown that the magnitude of placebo analgesia is generally *large* in studies that investigate placebo mechanisms (Price, Riley, & Vase, 2003; Vase et al., 2002; Vase, Petersen, Riley, & Price, 2009), and generally *low* in clinical trials that use placebo as a control condition (Hrobjartsson & Gotzsche, 2001, 2004, 2010). The average magnitude of placebo analgesia effects in placebo mechanisms studies is high as indicated by an average effect size of Cohen's $d = 1.00$ (Vase, Petersen, Riley, & Price, 2009), but the variation is large ($d = 0.12$–2.51) (see also Vase & Petersen, 2013). Only one meta-analysis has been conducted on the magnitude of nocebo hyperalgesia effects (Petersen, Finnerup, Colloca, et al., 2014), and it included only studies that investigated nocebo mechanisms. The average magnitude and variability of the nocebo effect was large and roughly similar to that of the placebo effect.

These meta-analyses are based on the existing literature which primarily involves studies with healthy volunteers. Interestingly, in the meta-analyses of placebo effects the largest magnitude of placebo analgesia was found in studies of chronic pain patients with hyperalgesia (Vase et al., 2009). In the meta-analysis of nocebo effects on the other hand, only one study involved chronic pain patients which is why general estimates of the magnitude of nocebo effects in hyperalgesic states cannot be made.

Verbal Suggestions for Pain Relief and Pain Increase

Several studies have demonstrated large placebo analgesia effects in chronic pain conditions (Kaptchuk et al., 2008, 2010; Klinger et al., 2007; Petersen et al., 2012; Price et al., 2007; Vase et al., 2003, 2005; Verne et al., 2003). Some of these studies have directly shown that adding a verbal suggestion for pain relief increases the magnitude of the placebo analgesia effect (Vase et al., 2003; Verne et al., 2003). This enhancement has been demonstrated in clinical trials in which IBS patients who were exposed to rectal distension received active treatment (lidocaine dissolved in a saline gel), placebo treatment (saline gel with or without overt placebo suggestion), or no treatment (saline gel with no placebo instructions) in a crossover fashion. In the first study, patients received an informed consent stating "this may be an active or an inactive agent," and a significant but moderate placebo effect was found (Verne et al., 2003). In the second study, the doctor added a verbal suggestion stating that "the agent you have just been given is known to significantly reduce pain in some patients," and a significant and very large placebo effect was found (Vase et al., 2003). Consistent with the different effects in these two studies, it has been demonstrated that the type of verbal suggestion influences the magnitude of the placebo analgesia effect (Pollo et al., 2001). Even more recent studies that used strong verbal suggestions for pain relief have shown large magnitudes of placebo analgesia effects (Kaptchuk et al., 2008, 2010; Price et al., 2007).

Recently, placebo effects have been investigated in chronic neuropathic pain patients receiving open and hidden administrations of the active agent lidocaine. In the open condition, lidocaine was applied to a disinfection napkin in full view of the patients and they were told "the agent you have just been given is known to powerfully reduce pain in some patients." In the hidden condition, lidocaine was applied to the napkin without the patients' knowledge and they were not given a verbal suggestion for pain relief. In the control condition, lidocaine was not applied to the napkin. The placebo effect was calculated as the difference in pain between the open and hidden administration of lidocaine, controlled for by a natural history condition (i.e., no treatment of the pain). A significant placebo effect was seen in spontaneous pain reports, as well as evoked types of pain such as area of hyperalgesia, pinprick hyperalgesia, and wind-up-like pain (Petersen et al., 2012; Petersen, Finnerup, Grosen, et al., 2014). In as far as only active medications were administered in these studies, this setting and the psychological processes that it gives rise to may resemble clinical practice to a higher extent than a traditional clinical trial.

At this point, only two studies have investigated nocebo effects in chronic pain patients. The first study involved IBS patients who in line with the clinical trial design outlined above, were exposed to rectal distension and tested during nocebo treatment (rectal lubricant along with nocebo suggestions) and no treatment (rectal lubricant and no suggestions). In the nocebo condition, the patients were told: "the agent you have just been given is known to significantly increase pain in some patients." The experienced pain was higher in the nocebo condition compared to the no treatment condition, but this difference was not significant (Vase et al., 2003). Recently, nocebo effects have been investigated in neuropathic pain patients where the patients received open versus hidden administrations of capsaicin controlled for the natural history of the pain in accordance with the study outlined above. In the open administration the patients were told "the agent you have just been given is known to powerfully increase pain in some patients." Similar to the IBS study by Vase et al. (2003) described above, there was a nonsignificant trend toward a nocebo effect (Petersen, Finnerup, Grosen, et al., 2014).

The absence of a significant nocebo effect in studies of chronic pain patients may be explained by several factors. First, researchers may be more reluctant to fully engage in verbal suggestions for pain increase as opposed to pain relief when testing chronic pain patients who already experience pain and discomfort. Also, patients who enter a hospital setting and establish a good relationship with a healthcare provider may have a harder time believing the negative verbal suggestions for pain increase. This circumstance may especially apply to the neuropathic pain patients mentioned in the study above, as most of these patients had not been in contact with doctors or the hospital with their pain problem prior to the study participation, so they did not have a history of pain treatment failure (Kessner, Wiech, Forkmann, Ploner, & Bingel, 2013).

Expectations and Emotional Feelings

Expected pain levels and emotional feelings are central to placebo effects and they have been shown to account for large amounts of the variance in placebo effects in chronic pain patients (Flaten et al., 2011, 2013; Price et al., 2008; Vase et al., 2003, 2004, 2005, 2011)

Expected pain levels are typically assessed by asking patients "what do you expect your pain level to be?" soon after the verbal suggestions for pain relief and treatment have been given and within 5 min before the treatment has taken effect. The patients subsequently indicate their expected pain level on a visual analog scale (VAS) ranging from "no pain" to the "worst pain imaginable" (Montgomery & Kirsch, 1997; Petersen et al., 2012; Price et al., 1999; Vase et al., 2003). In studies of IBS patients, expected pain levels along with the desire for pain relief have been shown to account for up to 81% of the variance in pain following inactive placebo and active lidocaine administration (Vase et al., 2003). In studies of neuropathic pain patients, expected pain levels have also contributed to experienced pain levels (Petersen, Finnerup, Grosen, et al., 2014).

Emotional feelings have traditionally been assessed by asking patients to indicate their level of positive and negative affect on the Positive and Negative Affect Scale (PANAS). The PANAS lists 20 predefined emotions such as being afraid and excited, and the positive affect scale generally reflects levels of enthusiasm and alertness, whereas the negative affect scale represents levels of subjective distress and unpleasurable engagement. The scale can be used to measure emotional feelings in general or in the present moment. In studies of neuropathic pain patients, a low score on the negative affect scale has been associated with a large placebo effect, whereas the positive affect scale has not been related to the placebo effect (Petersen et al., 2012). This is similar to findings in healthy volunteers (Scott et al., 2007).

Recently, however, it has been noted that the predefined emotions listed on the PANAS may only indirectly relate to the patients' actual experience in the present moment (Hurlburt, 2011). In order to understand how emotional feelings influence patients' ongoing clinical pain, it has been suggested to use the experiential method in which patients are directly asked about their personal experience in the moment when they knowingly receive a treatment (Price & Barrell, 2012; Vase et al., 2011). The experiential method was developed by Barrell and Price for the study of human experience by means of basic principles of phenomenology and psychometric methods (Price & Barrell, 1984, 2012). The purpose of the method is to understand the meaning of a given phenomenon in our experience and to preserve the vitality of the experience as it happens. Individuals are trained to notice brief episodes of direct experiences such as emotions and pain and to report these experiences without interpretations and explanations. The experiential reports are qualitatively sampled to determine the common elements within the experience and to characterize the interrelationship among them. The reports are also scaled using standard psychometric methods such as visual analog scales to investigate the intensity of the experiences and to see whether they support (other) quantitative data.

In a recent study of open versus hidden administrations of lidocaine and capsaicin, neuropathic pain patients were asked to relive their experience of placebo and nocebo interventions immediately after the treatment was administered and before it had taken effect. The patients were asked to quantitatively rate their emotional feelings on the VAS and to qualitatively describe these types of phenomenal experience in a few words (Petersen, Finnerup, Grosen, et al., 2014). Following the open administration of lidocaine, patients reported higher intensities of positive than negative emotions. These findings suggest that high levels of positive emotions and low levels of negative emotions are related to the pain experienced during the placebo intervention.

These findings stands in contrast to studies in which patients rated their position on predefined emotions via the PANAS and where only low levels of negative emotional feelings were related to pain levels during the placebo intervention. One explanation could be that patients do not necessarily experience the positive emotions as predefined in the PANAS, but instead as positive emotions that are captured by open reports of their immediate experience during a placebo intervention. By using the experiential method it also became clear that patients' expectations and emotional feelings were closely related as illustrated by a patient saying "I am hoping that the cream will bring relief." These findings are in line with a previous experiential study where patients' said "I am feeling pretty calm, I am not worried about anything because I am given something to affect my pain" (Vase et al., 2011). Thus when treating chronic pain patients it may be pivotal to keep in mind that the expectation of treatment effects are not neutral but are embedded in emotional feelings.

There was no significant nocebo effect in Petersen et al.'s study and patients reported similar levels of positive and negative emotional feelings during the nocebo condition. In contrast, predominantly positive emotional feelings occurred during the placebo condition.

Taken together, these findings illustrate that the experiential method may be useful in gaining a better understanding of patients' experiences during placebo and nocebo interventions. In the placebo intervention, it shows how expectations and emotional feelings are closely intertwined. In the nocebo intervention, it indicates that although patients experience negative emotional feelings, they do not exceed the positive emotional feelings. This supports the interpretation that the absence of significant nocebo effects may be due to the intervention not being perceived sufficiently harmful or unpleasant.

Clinical Implications

The studies outlined above show that placebo effects can be investigated in naturalistic settings in which healthcare providers openly give treatments to patients. They also suggest that the experiential method is a valuable approach to understanding patients' perception of a treatment, as well as their emotional feelings about and expectations of the treatment. Hence, these methods may be important contributions toward an understanding of how placebo and nocebo effects influence chronic pain patients' treatment outcomes in clinical practice.

Chronic pain patients often have a long history of treatment failures (Klinger & Flor, 2013). This treatment history is likely to influence not only the patients' expectations of future treatment outcome but also their emotional feelings about treatments. A landmark study of healthy volunteers has shown that verbal suggestions for pain increase may abolish the effect of well-documented pharmacological treatments (Bingel et al., 2011), thereby suggesting that expectations of pain increase can eliminate the efficacy of an analgesic treatment. The influence of negative expectations on the efficacy of active treatments for chronic pain patients in clinical practice has not yet been investigated. In future pharmacological studies of chronic pain patients it may thus be helpful to ask patients about their expectations and emotional feelings about treatments in order to understand how these psychological processes influence treatment outcomes.

When treating chronic pain patients in clinical practice, it appears important to directly ask patients about their expectations and emotional feelings in relation to a specific treatment. By openly initiating a conversion on this topic, it may become feasible to actively work with these psychological processes and to detect and alter, for example, unrealistic negative expectations and emotional feelings, which could hinder otherwise effective treatments from taking effect. Hence, active engagement in chronic pain patients' expectations and emotional feelings may have the potential to enhance the placebo components of therapies.

References

Benedetti, F. (2009). *Placebo effects: Understanding the mechanisms in health and disease*. Oxford, UK/New York, NY: Oxford University Press.

Bingel, U., Wanigasekera, V., Wiech, K., Ni Mhuircheartaigh, R., Lee, M. C., Ploner, M., & Tracey, I. (2011). The effect of treatment expectation on drug efficacy: Imaging the analgesic benefit of the opioid remifentanil. *Science Translational Medicine, 3*, 70ra14.

Colloca, L., Flaten, M. A., & Meissner, K. (2013). *Placebo and pain: From bench to bedside*. Burlington, MA: Elsevier.

Fields, H. L., & Price, D. D. (1997). Toward a neurobiology of placebo analgesia. In A. Harrington (Ed.), *The placebo effect. An interdisciplinary exploration* (pp. 93–116). Cambridge, MA: Harvard University Press.

Flaten, M. A., Aslaksen, P. M., & Lyby, P. S. (2013). Positive and negative emotions and placebo analgesia. In L. Colloca, M. Flaten, & K. Meissner (Eds.), *Placebo and pain: From bench to bedside* (pp. 73–81). Burlington, MA: Elsevier.

Flaten, M. A., Aslaksen, P. M., Lyby, P. S., & Bjorkedal, E. (2011). The relation of emotions to placebo responses. *Philosophical Transactions of the Royal Society of London B: Biological Sciences, 366*, 1818–1827.

Hrobjartsson, A., & Gotzsche, P. C. (2001). Is the placebo powerless? An analysis of clinical trials comparing placebo with no treatment. *The New England Journal of Medicine, 344*, 1594–1602.

Hrobjartsson, A., & Gotzsche, P. C. (2004). Is the placebo powerless? Update of a systematic review with 52 new randomized trials comparing placebo with no treatment. *Journal of Internal Medicine, 256*, 91–100.

Hrobjartsson, A., & Gotzsche, P. C. (2010). Placebo interventions for all clinical conditions. *The Cochrane Database of Systematic Reviews, 1*, CD003974. doi: 10.1002/14651858.CD003974.pub3

Hurlburt, R. T. (2011). *Investigating pristine inner experience: Moments of truth*. New York, NY: Cambridge University Press.

Hurlburt, R. T., & Heavey, C. L. (2001). Telling what we know: Describing inner experience. *Trends in Cognitive Sciences, 5*, 400–403.

Jensen, T. S., Dahl, J., & Arendt-Nielsen, L. (Eds.). (2013). *Smerter. Baggrund, evidens og behandling* [Pain. Background, evidence, and treatment]. Copenhagen, Denmark: FADLs.

Kaptchuk, T. J., Friedlander, E., Kelley, J. M., Sanchez, M. N., Kokkotou, E., Singer, J. P., ... Lembo, A. J. (2010). Placebos without deception: A randomized controlled trial in irritable bowel syndrome. *PloS One, 5*, e15591.

Kaptchuk, T. J., Kelley, J. M., Conboy, L. A., Davis, R. B., Kerr, C. E., Jacobson, E. E., ... Lembo, A. J. (2008). Components of placebo effect: Randomised controlled trial in patients with irritable bowel syndrome. *BMJ (Clinical Research Ed.), 336*, 999–1003.

Kessner, S., Wiech, K., Forkmann, K., Ploner, M., & Bingel, U. (2013). The effect of treatment history on therapeutic outcome: An experimental approach. *JAMA Internal Medicine, 173*, 1468–1469.

Klinger, R., & Flor, H. (2013). The potential of the analgesic placebo effect in clinical practice–recommendations for pain management. In L. Colloca, M. Flaten, & K. Meissner (Eds.), *Placebo and pain: From bench to bedside* (pp. 267–275). Burlington, MA: Elsevier.

Klinger, R., Soost, S., Flor, H., & Worm, M. (2007). Classical conditioning and expectancy in placebo hypoalgesia: A randomized controlled study in patients with atopic dermatitis and persons with healthy skin. *Pain, 128*, 31–39.

Montgomery, G. H., & Kirsch, I. (1997). Classical conditioning and the placebo effect. *Pain, 72*, 107–113.

Petersen, G.L., Finnerup, N.B., Colloca, L., Amanzio, M., Price, D. D., Jensen, T.S., & Vase, L. (2014). The magnitude of nocebo effects in pain: A meta-analysis. *Pain*. Advance online publication. doi: 10.1016/j.pain.2014.04.016.

Petersen, G. L., Finnerup, N. B., Grosen, K., Pilegaard, H. K., Tracey, I., Benedetti, F., . . . Vase, L. (2014). *Expectations and positive emotional feelings accompany reductions of decrease in ongoing and evoked neuropathic pain following placebo interventions*. Manuscript in preparation.

Petersen, G. L., Finnerup, N. B., Norskov, K. N., Grosen, K., Pilegaard, H. K., Benedetti, F., . . . Vase, L. (2012). Placebo manipulations reduce hyperalgesia in neuropathic pain. *Pain, 153*, 1292–1300.

Piche, M., Bouin, M., Arsenault, M., Poitras, P., & Rainville, P. (2011). Decreased pain inhibition in irritable bowel syndrome depends on altered descending modulation and higher-order brain processes. *Neuroscience, 195*, 166–175.

Pollo, A., Amanzio, M., Arslanian, A., Casadio, C., Maggi, G., & Benedetti, F. (2001). Response expectancies in placebo analgesia and their clinical relevance. *Pain, 93*, 77–84.

Price, D. D. (1999). *Psychological mechanisms of pain and analgesia*. Seattle, WA: IASP Press.

Price, D. D., & Barrell, J. J. (1984). Some general laws of human emotion: Interrelationships between intensities of desire, expectation and emotional feeling. *Journal of Personality, 52*, 389–409.

Price, D. D., & Barrell, J. J. (2012). *Inner experience and neuroscience: Merging both perspectives*. Cambridge, MA: MIT Press.

Price, D. D., Craggs, J., Verne, G. N., Perlstein, W. M., & Robinson, M. E. (2007). Placebo analgesia is accompanied by large reductions in pain-related brain activity in irritable bowel syndrome patients. *Pain, 127*, 63–72.

Price, D. D., Finniss, D. G., & Benedetti, F. (2008). A comprehensive review of the placebo effect: Recent advances and current thought. *Annual Review of Psychology, 59*, 565–590.

Price, D. D., Milling, L. S., Kirsch, I., Duff, A., Montgomery, G. H., & Nicholls, S. S. (1999). An analysis of factors that contribute to the magnitude of placebo analgesia in an experimental paradigm. *Pain, 83*, 147–156.

Price, D. D., Riley, J. L. III, & Vase, L. (2003). Reliable differences in placebo effects between clinical analgesic trials and studies of placebo analgesia mechanisms. *Pain, 104*, 715–716.

Price, D. D., & Vase, L. (2013). The contribution of Desire, Expectation and Reduced Negative Emotions to Placebo Anti-hyperalgesia in Irritable Bowel Syndrome. In L. Colloca, M. Flaten, & K. Meissner (Eds.), *Placebo and pain: From bench to bedside* (pp. 215–26). Burlington, MA: Elsevier.

Scott, D. J., Stohler, C. S., Egnatuk, C. M., Wang, H., Koeppe, R. A., & Zubieta, J. K. (2007). Individual differences in reward responding explain placebo-induced expectations and effects. *Neuron, 55*, 325–336.

Vase, L., Norskov, K. N., Petersen, G. L., & Price, D. D. (2011). Patients' direct experiences as central elements of placebo analgesia. *Philosophical Transactions of the Royal Society of London B: Biological Sciences, 366*, 1913–1921.

Vase, L., & Petersen, G. L. (2013). Conceptualization and magnitudes of placebo analgesia effects across meta-analyses and experimental studies. In L. Colloca, M. Flaten, & K. Meissner (Eds.), *Placebo and pain: From bench to bedside* (pp. 203–213). Burlington, MA: Elsevier.

Vase, L., Petersen, G. L., Riley, J. L. 3rd, & Price, D. D. (2009). Factors contributing to large analgesic effects in placebo mechanism studies conducted between 2002 and 2007. *Pain, 145*, 36–44.

Vase, L., Price, D. D., Verne, G. N., & Robinson, M. E. (2004). The contribution on changes in expected pain levels and desire for pain relief to placebo analgesia. In D. D. Price & M. C. Bushnell (Eds.), *Psychological methods of pain control: Basic science and clinical perspectives* (pp. 207–234). Seattle, WA: IASP Press.

Vase, L., Riley, J. L. 3rd, & Price, D. D. (2002). A comparison of placebo effects in clinical analgesic trials versus studies of placebo analgesia. *Pain, 99*, 443–452.

Vase, L., Robinson, M. E., Verne, G. N., & Price, D. D. (2003). The contributions of suggestion, desire, and expectation to placebo effects in irritable bowel syndrome patients. An empirical investigation. *Pain, 105*, 17–25.

Vase, L., Robinson, M. E., Verne, G. N., & Price, D. D. (2005). Increased placebo analgesia over time in irritable bowel syndrome (IBS) patients is associated with desire and expectation but not endogenous opioid mechanisms. *Pain, 115*, 338–347.

Verne, G. N., Robinson, M. E., Vase, L., & Price, D. D. (2003). Reversal of visceral and cutaneous hyperalgesia by local rectal anesthesia in irritable bowel syndrome (IBS) patients. *Pain, 105*, 223–230.

Lene Vase

Department of Psychology and Behavioral Sciences
School of Business and Social Sciences
Aarhus University
Bartholins Alle 16
8000 Aarhus C
Denmark
Tel. +45 8716-5828
Fax +45 8716-4401
E-mail lenevase@psy.au.dk

Review Article

How to Psychologically Minimize Scratching Impulses

Benefits of Placebo Effects on Itching Using Classical Conditioning and Expectancy

Ariane Sölle,[1] Theresa Bartholomäus,[2] Margitta Worm,[2] and Regine Klinger[1]

[1]Outpatient Clinic of Behavior Therapy, Department of Psychology, University of Hamburg, Germany,
[2]Hospital for Dermatology, Venereology und Allergology, Allergy Center, Charité University Medicine, Berlin, Germany

Abstract. Research in recent years, especially in the analgesic field, has intensively studied the placebo effect and its mechanisms. It has been shown that physical complaints can be efficiently reduced via learning and cognitive processes (conditioning and expectancies). However, despite evidence demonstrating a large variety of physiological similarities between pain and itch, the possible transfer of the analgesic placebo model to itch has not yet been widely discussed in research. This review therefore aims at highlighting potential transfers of placebo mechanisms to itch processes by demonstrating the therapeutic issues in pharmacological treatments for pruritus on a physiological basis and by discussing the impact of psychological mechanisms and psychological factors influencing itch sensations.

Keywords: itching, psychological factors, conditioning, placebo effect

Itch is an irritating and major symptom of many chronic skin diseases such as atopic eczema, psoriasis, and urticaria (Verhoeven et al., 2007). It has been defined as a sensation provoking a scratching impulse or the need to scratch (Savin, 1998) and this, in turn, has a strong effect on the patients' quality of life (Erturk, Arican, Omurlu, & Sut, 2012; Verhoeven et al., 2007; Weisshaar & Dalgard, 2009).

Unfortunately, present evidence indicates that the efficacy of the drugs currently used to overcome itching can be highly variable (Yosipovitch & Papoiu, 2008). However, under certain circumstances such variance might be attributed to different characteristics in the placebo effectiveness. In the field of analgesic treatments, conditioning and expectancy processes have enhanced the pain-reducing effects of analgesic medication (Klinger, Soost, Flor, & Worm, 2007). Due to the substantial similarity between pain and pruritus with regard to their mode of action (Depenau et al., 2012; Ikoma, Steinhoff, Ständer, Yosipovitch, & Schmelz, 2006), it seems reasonable to transfer the analgesic placebo model to the concept of itching and to discuss the benefits of its psychological mechanisms. Analgesic medication is suggested to be made up of two components: The pure pharmacological versus the psychological component, whereby the latter can be termed: *additive placebo effect.* It is assumed to enhance the pure pharmacological effects of drugs and thereby increase the analgesic medical efficacy within ethical limitations (Benedetti, 2008). Consequently, if anti-itching drugs could systematically be amplified with an additional placebo effect using psychological mechanisms, this would have very positive therapeutic implications.

The present article aims at discussing the current state of placebo effect research by focusing on the physiological and psychological aspects of itch that seem to be similar to pain. This review will demonstrate the therapeutic issues in pharmacological treatments for pruritus in order to identify and propose some ideas leading to experimental approaches of great clinical relevance.

Impact of Placebo Effects on Pruritus Treatment

Placebo effects are generally defined as a response following a placebo application which is completely inert. It is crucial to point out that the procedures used in these inert interventions, which provoke placebo responses, are always limited to verbal suggestions, the context in which the treatment is presented, and to learning experiences (e.g., in the case of analgesic placebo effects, they refer to the association between placebo and pain reduction). These factors lead to a patient's confidence in the intervention as an effective and trustworthy therapy. Consequently, the placebo effect, as an additive non-pharmacological benefit in therapy, depends on many elements involved in the patient's surroundings. These environmental treatment factors affect their desires, experiences, and expectancies toward therapeutic outcomes (Benedetti, 2008; Finniss, Kaptchuk, Miller, & Benedetti, 2010).

The current treatment of pruritus mainly consists of antihistamines in addition to corticosteroids, but findings suggest a very high variance in their efficacy (Hosogi, Schmelz, Miyachi, & Ikoma, 2006; Ikoma, Handwerker, Miyachi, & Schmelz, 2005; Klein & Clark, 1999; Yosipovitch & Papoiu, 2008). Despite existing debates over a histamine-induced itch, antihistamines remain the most frequently used drugs in itch treatment of atopic dermatitis (AD) (Herman & Vender, 2003). Against this backdrop and many other underlying controversially discussed physiological mechanisms of pruritus, the question whether we could deliberately improve the efficacy of itch treatment by applying the placebo mechanisms, could have a profound impact.

Substantial evidence for using placebo effects in allergic treatments is provided by a meta-analysis focusing on longitudinal results of allergen-specific immunotherapies (Narkus et al., 2013). The findings indicate a high placebo efficacy in patients over a 2-year-period. This effect was more prominent in subcutaneous therapy trials than in trials with sublingual applications, indicating that the method of administration plays an important role in establishing placebo responses. Further meta-analyses using placebo-controlled studies support the efficacy of placebo responses in inflammatory diseases. For instance, another study also covering allergic reactions (e.g., allergic rhinitis, allergic asthma, AD) demonstrated average placebo effects of 23% in a placebo-controlled medication design (e.g., antihistamines) (Narkus et al., 2013; Radziwill & Kruszewski, 2011). The existence of not intentionally triggered placebo effects in studies, which used placebos as controls for medication, is an important clue when considering the enlargement of the placebo effect via directed psychological mechanisms.

Mechanisms of Placebo Effects in Pruritus Treatments – Are They Transferable From Placebo Analgesia?

Psychological Mechanisms of Placebo Effects

In addition to many other psychological influences, two explanatory theories have been suggested for achieving placebo effects: The expectancy and the classical conditioning model (Price, Finniss, & Benedetti, 2008). The expectancy model refers to the experience of placebo effects by giving instructions which increase positive expectations of the patient toward the treatment (Kirsch, 1985; Montgomery & Kirsch, 1997; Pollo et al., 2001; Voudouris, Peck, & Coleman, 1990). The second proposed theory involves classical conditioning effects (Siegel, 2002): A neutral stimulus (e.g., represented by the shape, color, size of an inert pill) is presented together with an unconditioned stimulus (e.g., the pharmacological effect of a drug) which leads to an associated link between these two conditions. Thus, the neutral stimulus becomes a conditioned stimulus leading to similar effects to those of the pharmacological drug (Benedetti, 2008).

Research findings suggest that expectations might be more involved in conscious aspects, whereas conditioning aspects are implicated to subconscious processing of placebo responses, such as immune responses (Benedetti et al., 2003). However, further research has demonstrated the inclusion of both concepts to explain pain-, itch-relieving (Klinger et al., 2007), and immunomodulatory placebo effects (Pacheco-López, Engler, Niemi, & Schedlowski, 2006; Schedlowski & Pacheco-López, 2010).

Furthermore, investigations focusing on observational and social learning have shown that observing analgesic placebo effects in other persons leads to a reduced experience of pain in subsequent experimental pain measurements. These experienced placebo responses were comparable to the benefits gained by conditioning and verbal suggestions (Colloca & Benedetti, 2009). Additionally, several studies have shown that the social context influences the outcome of the placebo effect, indicating that a convincing, positive patient-doctor-interaction affects the state of health favorably (Colloca, Lopiano, Lanotte, & Benedetti, 2004; Colloca & Miller, 2011; Kaptchuk et al., 2008; Miller, Colloca, & Kaptchuk, 2009).

It has already been shown that the described placebo responses are very effective in many diseases (Finniss et al., 2010; Kirsch, 2000; Vase, Robinson, Verne, & Price, 2003). In particular, analgesic research indicates an additive effect to pharmaceuticals via underlying psychological mechanisms in pain treatment (Vase, Riley, & Price, 2002). Moreover, it has led to the implementation of therapeutic guidelines in pain management, recommending the maximization of the placebo effect in perioperative treatments (Klinger, 2010; Klinger, Thomm, Bryant, & Becker, 2008).

A recent investigation comparing itch and pain sensations has revealed that verbal suggestions in experimental settings manipulate expectations and lead to altered itching and pain (Van Laarhoven et al., 2011). The study included healthy participants who first took part in an experimental nocebo condition followed by an experimental placebo condition. The findings show that, with regard to the nocebo condition, preliminary verbal instructions inducing high expectations of experiencing itch did lead to increased itch sensations compared to the suggestions encouraging low expectations of itching. Sensation measurements were always conducted after monofilament stimulation, electrical stimulation, and histamine iontophoresis, asking the participants to rate the personally perceived itch sensation. The results of the data focusing on suggestions which induced pain-increasing expectancies also highlighted higher pain levels but these nocebo effects were not as strong as in the itch conditions. In the placebo conditions, participants either informed that a substance added to the applied gel would definitely lead to reduced itching, or that almost all people experience itch sensations from the administered stimuli (only histamine iontophoresis). The outcomes indicated no differences in itch perception between these two groups, leading to no expected placebo effect. Similar results were found in the groups experiencing pain. However, previous research has highlighted that achieving placebo effects is a combination of induced expectations and conditioning (Colloca & Benedetti, 2006; Colloca, Petrovic, Wager, Ingvar, & Benedetti, 2010; Colloca, Sigaudo, & Benedetti, 2008; Klinger et al., 2007).

In one of these studies, electrical pain-inducing stimuli were applied to AD patients and healthy participants in a clinical setting. The intensity of the induced pain was reduced in a conditioning section after an ointment had been applied. The inert ointment was either labeled as neutral or as pain-relieving. The findings of this study showed that both expectancies and classical conditioning led to decreased pain perception, the so-called placebo effect. Moreover, the data suggest that lasting effects were attributed to a combination of these psychological modes of action. Interestingly, the data also indicated that conditioning in AD helped to maintain the placebo effect compared to unconditioned AD patients, whereas conditioning led to no differences in the placebo effect for healthy controls. In conclusion, it was suggested that patients attached more importance to the outcome of therapies and were therefore more vulnerable to the given verbal information (Klinger et al., 2007; Klinger, Colloca, Bingel, & Flor, 2014). Supporting evidence has revealed that dedicating attention to stimuli influences the intensity of sensation outcomes (Van Laarhoven, Kraaimaat, Wilder-Smith, & Evers, 2010).

The presented research findings from current studies on the placebo effect in pruritus, demonstrate the lack of evidence explaining placebo responses behind itching processes. It has been shown that, as for pain, negative expectations generated through verbal suggestions led to nocebo effects. However, the positive side of the expectancy theory and the conditioning aspect, the achieved placebo effect, could only be shown via pain-inducing stimuli in AD patients. One further critical aspect is that the existing current placebo research on itch mainly covers studies on healthy participants. It may be, and it has already been suggested in Klinger et al. (2007), that patients with skin diseases must be differentiated from healthy participants due to the patients' increased desire for symptom reduction (Colloca & Miller, 2011), whereby the term *desire* involves motivational aspects for symptom reduction and is closely linked to the patient's confidence in treatment (Price & Fields, 1997).

Psychological Factors Influencing Placebo Responses

Especially in the field of placebo analgesia, it has already been shown that cognitive factors, like attention (Aldrich, Eccleston, & Crombez, 2000; Crombez, Van Damme, & Eccleston, 2005; Van Damme, Legrain, Vogt, & Crombez, 2010), emotions (Weisenberg, Raz, & Hener, 1998; Wiech & Tracey, 2009), stress and the construct "desire" (Klinger et al., 2007), have a profound impact on pain sensations (Benedetti, 2008; Price et al., 2008). However, their role in the placebo effect on itch has not yet been systematically investigated, though the available evidence suggests that worrying and negative expectations are associated with the therapeutic outcome and with increased itch intensities (Scholz & Hermanns, 1994; Verhoeven et al., 2008). Moreover, early findings from an observational study have shown that a pruritus-inducing lecture provoked itch sensations in the listeners (Niemeier, Kupfer, & Gieler, 2000). However, the results are based on healthy volunteers and it may be assumed that patients display more attentional bias to itch-related information than controls. Associated findings from psoriasis research support this suggestion (Fortune et al., 2003) as does a recent study by Van Laarhoven et al. (2010). The latter used somatosensory (pain- and itch-inducing) stimuli in order to test whether patients with chronic pain or itch show a greater attentional focus on pain or on pruritus. Interestingly, the results highlighted not only the positive link between attention and itch/pain perception, but also indicated that increased attention levels were associated with higher levels of experienced itch.

Due to the link between the evoked negative expectancies and their influence on body sensation as described above, there might also be a relationship between emotions and bodily symptoms. For example, some analgesic research indicates that people experiencing fear of pain do not respond positively to placebos. However, strengthening strategies for counteracting negative emotions and stress, increases the activity of opioid systems, which, in turn, is also associated with attaining placebo effects (Flaten, Aslaksen, Lyby, & Bjørkedal, 2011). Additionally, evidence shows that reducing anxiety may enhance improved immune responses (Turner, Deyo, Loeser, Von Korff, & Fordyce, 1994). There are not many findings from pruritus research, although it has been shown that negative emotions are correlated with itch perception (Van Laarhoven et al., 2012) in inflammatory diseases (Conrad et al., 2008; Verhoeven et al., 2009), and in one study more than three-fourths (81%) of AD patients stated that emotional stress compounded their itch perception (Buddenkotte & Steinhoff, 2010; Wahlgren, 1992).

Physiological Mediators and Mechanisms

It is important to point out that there are many psychological factors that might influence a patient's state of health, so that the recent evidence do not refer to one single placebo effect but rather to different systems and mechanisms influenced by and contributing to many different placebo effects (Benedetti, 2008; Enck, Benedetti, & Schedlowski, 2008).

Equally, a large range of mediators such as peripheral and central ones have been suggested to be involved in the pathogenesis of pruritus. One of the promising concepts behind itching processes is the transfer of pain to itch. Based on analgesic research, endogenous opioid mechanisms are most often considered as being involved in placebo responses (Benedetti, 2008; Finniss et al., 2010). A wide variety of evidence including neuroimaging techniques (Eippert et al., 2009; Zubieta et al., 2005) as well as investigations with the opioid antagonist naloxone (Benedetti, 1996; Levine & Gordon, 1984; Levine, Gordon, & Fields, 1978), confirmed the mediation by an endogenous opioid system. The clinical management of pruritus also indicates the peripheral and central treatment of itch via endogenous opioid mechanisms (Tey & Yosipovitch, 2011). It has been suggested that kappa-opioid-agonists and topically used preparations of opioid receptor antagonists and agonists inhibit itching processes (Bigliardi et al., 2007; Phan, Lotts, Antal, Bernhard, & Ständer, 2012). However, there is also strong evidence that many opioid receptor agonists and antagonists which are useful for the reduction of pain actually enhance itch (Ikoma et al., 2006; McRae et al., 2003). Future research will need to address this important issue in greater detail.

Another approach gaining in relevance is the specificity theory (McMahon & Koltzenburg, 1992), which posits separate afferent pathways for pain and itch, has become more influential because of research showing that itch sensation may be the result of mechanically insensitive C-fibers responding to induced histamine and connecting to the posterior horn and thalamus (Ikoma, 2013; Ikoma et al., 2006; Schmelz, Schmidt, Bickel, Handwerker, & Torebjörk, 1997; Schmelz et al., 2000). Additionally, it has been shown that these histamine-sensitive C-fibers might also be weakly activated by pain-inducing substances such as capsaicin and bradykinin (Ikoma, Cevikbas, Kempkes, & Steinhoff, 2011; Schmelz et al., 2003). In contrast, the most frequent types of C-fibers in skin nerves are described as polymodal and responding to mechanical, thermal, and chemical stimuli, including weak activation via histamines (Ikoma et al., 2005; Schmelz, 2002). Consequently, this recent research considers histamine-sensitive C-fibers as being rather selective (Ikoma et al., 2011).

When considering the similarities between pain and itch, the available evidence also suggest and indicate that endogenic inflammatory mediators activate both nociceptors and pruriceptors (Kidd & Urban, 2001; Schmelz, 2005; Schmelz et al., 2003). For example, Toyoda and colleagues (2002) have shown a correlation between the pain-related parameters Nerve Growth Factor (NGF) (Yamaguchi, Aihara, Kobayashi, Kambara, & Ikezawa, 2009), Substance P (SP) and the severity of AD. Moreover, there are also evidence indicating reduced levels of Calcitonin-Gene-Related-Peptide (CGRP) in inflammatory diseases in rats (Katsuno et al., 2003), whereas these neuropeptide levels seem to be increased in pain-related processes (Mogil et al., 2005).

Stress and pruritus are also closely linked. Research findings have shown that stress enhances itching via complex neuronal mechanisms (Pavlovic et al., 2008). For instance, a study on rodents indicated a positive correlation between stress and mast cell degranulation (Singh, Pang, Alexacos, Letourneau, & Theoharides, 1999) encouraging the suggestion that stress may lead to raised levels of pruritogenic agents in AD patients (Buddenkotte & Steinhoff, 2010; Fjellner, Arnetz, Eneroth, & Kallner, 1985; Liezmann, Klapp, & Peters, 2011). Furthermore, studies with AD patients have demonstrated that highly negative information about the outcome prior to histamine prick testing led to increased itch perceptions (Scholz & Hermanns, 1994). In placebo research too, there is a suggestion that the mode of action of placebo responses via stress and anxiety reduction might be reasonable. Consequently, if stress influences pruritus sensations, the efficacy of itch-relieving placebos might be explainable via stress reduction (Kim & Yosipovitch, 2013).

The complexity of itch and the high variance of its medical treatments might be caused by the large variety of peripheral mediators and neuronal mechanisms involved. The available recent research described in this paper proposes a neurobiological overlap between pain and itch with regard to their mechanisms. For a detailed neurobiological review on pain and itch, see Ikoma et al. (2006). On the other hand, a link between the immune system and placebo responses in inflammatory diseases (which includes pruritus) has also been proposed (Ader et al., 2010; Narkus et al., 2013; Pacheco-López et al., 2006; Yosipovitch & Papoiu, 2008).

Consequently, the transfer of the already well-established placebo effect mechanism "conditioning" depends on its systems, its mechanisms and their mediators, which should be conditioned. As antihistamines are frequently used in pharmaceutical itch treatments, the mediator histamine may be assumed to be a promising parameter for evoking placebo responses through conditioning. Future research should focus on how placebo effects could be deliberately maximized in clinical settings in order to reduce unpleasant itch sensations.

Impact of Placebo Effects Within Ethical Boundaries

The present article has provided a brief overview of the similarities between pain and itch, thus reasoning the transfer of the analgesic placebo model to pruritus in order to explain how underlying psychological mechanisms can also account for explanations concerning itch processes. The physiological basis on which these mechanisms might occur has not been sufficiently investigated and further research is needed. Nevertheless, the transfer of the analgesic placebo model to clinical settings treating itch sensations is assumed to be beneficial and the additive placebo model of Benedetti (2008) provides an especially promising approach. Here, the placebo effect is the additive non-pharmacological benefit to a drug resulting in the overall efficacy to a treatment, as illustrated in Figure 1. For instance, an antihistamine might have a pharmacological effect, which has been described as highly variable (Yosipovitch & Papoiu, 2008), and a

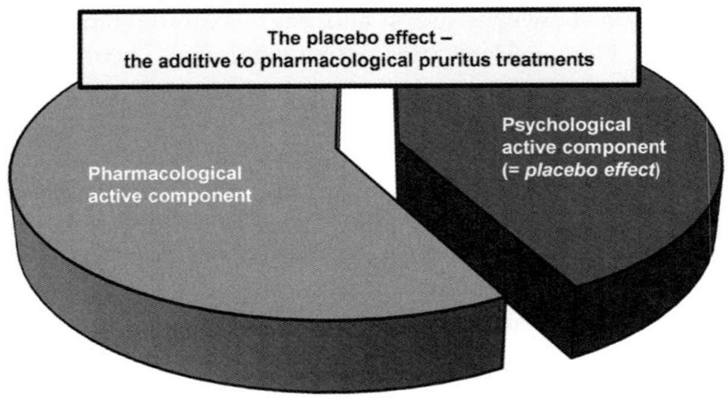

Figure 1. The additive placebo effect. The efficacy of drugs consists of the pure pharmacological treatment and the psychological component (placebo effect).

psychologically evoked additional benefit – the so-called placebo effect.

In conclusion, drug treatments such as administering antihistamines can be optimized by including psychological context variables. In order to test these effects, different characteristics of pharmacological treatment should be considered in clinical settings:

- Requested treatment: The positive aspects of pruritus-reducing medication (e.g., antihistamines) should be emphasized, realistic effects of the drugs are explained to patients and side effects are not overrated.
- Patients are informed about the purpose of the drug (e.g., reducing itch) but further information is not provided.
- A drug can be administered hidden (e.g., via drug infusion pumps) so that the patients are unaware of the treatment (Levine & Gordon, 1984).

Several analgesia studies have investigated the open-hidden paradigm, in which a treatment is either fully accessible to patients or hidden. This means that patients receive treatments without any cues (Price et al., 2008). This evidence indicates that open pharmaceutical administration is more effective than the hidden form (Amanzio, Pollo, Maggi, & Benedetti, 2001; Benedetti et al., 2003; Colloca et al., 2004).

For instance, it has been found that openly administered analgesics (drug is directly given by the doctor to the patient) required lower doses of the drug in order to reach the same analgesic effect as in a hidden setting (the patient is unaware of receiving the drug which is given via an infusion pump) (Amanzio et al., 2001). Thus, the difference between the outcomes of open (with expectancies factors) and hidden administration (none expectancy) reflects the placebo effect as a psychological component (Colloca & Benedetti, 2005).

Adopting this open-hidden-paradigm in future research of placebo effects on chronic itch patients should be of great clinical relevance, because placebo effects in treatment can be administered without deception aspects, which have already been reviewed in detail in the literature (Miller & Colloca, 2011).

A suitable research design for investigating placebo effects in itch should therefore include this open-hidden paradigm. The "open" applications of an itch-reducing medication can be differentiated. For instance, there can be an advanced open drug administration (instructions emphasizing the positive aspect of antihistamines combined with conditioning) or the administration can be reduced to verbal suggestions (only instructions). Next to these groups (2× open, 1× hidden), it would also be of high clinical interest to compare the described open drug applications (instructions, with/without conditioning) with a placebo application (instructions and/or conditioning, inert substance). A placebo application without these psychological mechanisms would be a hidden placebo which is not of clinical interest.

Preliminary data on AD patients (see Figure 2) shows that the described non-full-factorial design seems to be

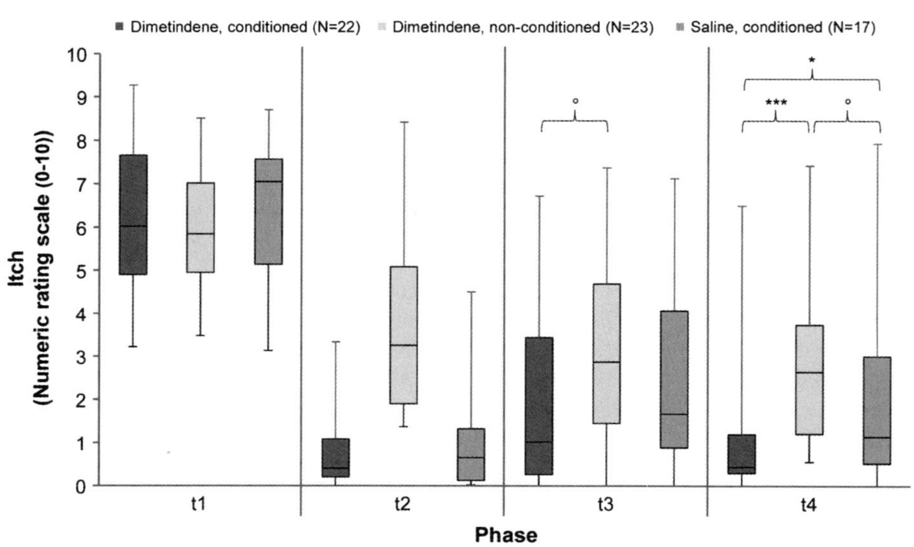

Figure 2. Conditioning effects on pruritic sensations in AD patients in addition to antihistamine administration (preliminary data). Measurement of experimentally induced itch sensation on a numeric rating scale at three time points (t1 = baseline, t3, t4). The conditioning was carried out by inducing fewer itch sensations at t2. Alpha was adjusted via Bonferroni correction (° marginally significant ($p < .033$), *significant ($p < .017$), ***highly significant ($p < .0003$)).

suitable for investigating itch sensations. All patient groups (conditioned antihistamine-receiving group, a non-conditioned group and a conditioned saline-receiving placebo group) received verbal suggestions and experienced reduced itch sensations compared to the baseline measurement (t1); however the groups undergoing a classical conditioning process (less induced itch in t2) showed a significantly greater decrease in itch sensations compared to the non-conditioned antihistamine-group (t3, t4).

Conclusions

In the past years, research has broadened our understanding of the mechanisms that underlie pruritus. Due to the large range of mediators and mechanisms contributing to the development of itch which have consequently yielded a high variance of the efficacy of anti-itching-drugs, this review aimed at showing how research could focus on psychological mechanisms in combination with medication in order to improve pruritus therapies. The additive placebo effect seems to play an important role in pain relief, a symptom which bears resemblance to itch sensations, so that the transfer of placebo models should be more extensively investigated in itch processes, especially in clinical settings.

Acknowledgments

This work was supported by the German Research Foundation under grants KL 1350/5-1 and WO 541/14-1.

References

Ader, R., Mercurio, M. G., Walton, J., James, D., Davis, M., Ojha, V., . . . Fiorentino, D. (2010). Conditioned pharmacotherapeutic effects: A preliminary study. *Psychosomatic Medicine, 72*, 192–197.

Aldrich, S., Eccleston, C., & Crombez, G. (2000). Worrying about chronic pain: Vigilance to threat and misdirected problem solving. *Behaviour Research and Therapy, 38*, 457–470.

Amanzio, M., Pollo, A., Maggi, G., & Benedetti, F. (2001). Response variability to analgesics: A role for non-specific activation of endogenous opioids. *Pain, 90*, 205–215.

Benedetti, F. (1996). The opposite effects of the opiate antagonist naloxone and the cholecystokinin antagonist proglumide on placebo analgesia. *Pain, 64*, 535–543.

Benedetti, F. (2008). Mechanisms of placebo and placebo-related effects across diseases and treatments. *Annual Review of Pharmacology and Toxicology, 48*, 33–60.

Benedetti, F., Pollo, A., Lopiano, L., Lanotte, M., Vighetti, S., & Rainero, I. (2003). Conscious expectation and unconscious conditioning in analgesic, motor, and hormonal placebo/nocebo responses. *Journal of Neuroscience, 23*, 4315–4323.

Bigliardi, P. L., Stammer, H., Jost, G., Rufli, T., Büchner, S., & Bigliardi-Qi, M. (2007). Treatment of pruritus with topically applied opiate receptor antagonist. *Journal of the American Academy of Dermatology, 56*, 979–988.

Buddenkotte, J., & Steinhoff, M. (2010). Pathophysiology and therapy of pruritus in allergic and atopic diseases. *Allergy, 65*, 805–821.

Colloca, L., & Benedetti, F. (2005). Placebos and painkillers: Is mind as real as matter? *Nature Reviews Neuroscience, 6*, 545–552.

Colloca, L., & Benedetti, F. (2006). How prior experience shapes placebo analgesia. *Pain, 124*, 126–133.

Colloca, L., & Benedetti, F. (2009). Placebo analgesia induced by social observational learning. *Pain, 144*, 28–34.

Colloca, L., Lopiano, L., Lanotte, M., & Benedetti, F. (2004). Overt versus covert treatment for pain, anxiety, and Parkinson's disease. *The Lancet, 3*, 679–684.

Colloca, L., & Miller, F. G. (2011). How placebo responses are formed: A learning perspective. *Philosophical transactions of the Royal Society of London. Series B: Biological sciences, 366*, 1859–1869.

Colloca, L., Petrovic, P., Wager, T. D., Ingvar, M., & Benedetti, F. (2010). How the number of learning trials affects placebo and nocebo responses. *Pain, 151*, 430–439.

Colloca, L., Sigaudo, M., & Benedetti, F. (2008). The role of learning in nocebo and placebo effects. *Pain, 136*, 211–218.

Conrad, R., Geiser, F., Haidl, G., Hutmacher, M., Liedtke, R., & Wermter, F. (2008). Relationship between anger and pruritus perception in patients with chronic idiopathic urticaria and psoriasis. *Journal of the European Academy of Dermatology and Venereology, 22*, 1062–1069.

Crombez, G., Van Damme, S., & Eccleston, C. (2005). Hypervigilance to pain: An experimental and clinical analysis. *Pain, 116*, 4–7.

Depenau, C., Schröder, R., Osada, N., Baron, R., Schmelz, M., Pogatzki-Zahn, E., & Ständer, S. (2012). Schmerzen und Jucken: Unterschiede und Gemeinsamkeiten veranschaulicht anhand von per PainDetect-Fragebogen erhobenen Parametern [Pain and pruritus: Differences and similarities as revealed by the PainDetect questionnaire parameters]. *Der Hautarzt, 63*, 539–546. doi: 10.1007/s00105-011-2322-7

Eippert, F., Bingel, U., Schoell, E. D., Yacubian, J., Klinger, R., Lorenz, J., & Büchel, C. (2009). Activation of the opioidergic descending pain control system underlies placebo analgesia. *Neuron, 63*, 533–543.

Enck, P., Benedetti, F., & Schedlowski, M. (2008). New insights into the placebo and nocebo responses. *Neuron, 59*, 195–206.

Erturk, I. E., Arican, O., Omurlu, I. K., & Sut, N. (2012). Effect of the pruritus on the quality of life: A preliminary study. *Annals of Dermatology, 24*, 406–412.

Finniss, D. G., Kaptchuk, T. J., Miller, F., & Benedetti, F. (2010). Biological, clinical, and ethical advances of placebo effects. *Lancet, 375*, 686–695.

Fjellner, B., Arnetz, B. B., Eneroth, P., & Kallner, A. (1985). Pruritus during standardized mental stress. Relationship to psychoneuroendocrine and metabolic parameters. *Acta Dermato-Venereologica, 65*, 199–205.

Flaten, M. A., Aslaksen, P. M., Lyby, P. S., & Bjørkedal, E. (2011). The relation of emotions to placebo responses. *Philosophical transactions of the Royal Society of London. Series B: Biological sciences, 366*, 1818–1827.

Fortune, D. G., Richards, H. L., Corrin, A., Taylor, R. J., Griffiths, C. E., & Main, C. J. (2003). Attentional bias for psoriasis-specific and psychosocial threat in patients with psoriasis. *Journal of Behavioral Medicine, 26*, 211–224.

Herman, S. M., & Vender, R. B. (2003). Antihistamines in the treatment of atopic dermatitis. *Journal of Cutaneous Medicine and Surgery: Incorporating Medical and Surgical Dermatology, 7*, 467–473.

Hosogi, M., Schmelz, M., Miyachi, Y., & Ikoma, A. (2006). Bradykinin is a potent pruritogen in atopic dermatitis: A switch from pain to itch. *Pain, 126*, 16–23.

Ikoma, A. (2013). Updated neurophysiology of itch. *Biological & Pharmaceutical Bulletin, 36*, 1235–1240.

Ikoma, A., Cevikbas, F., Kempkes, C., & Steinhoff, M. (2011). Anatomy and neurophysiology of pruritus. *Seminars in Cutaneous Medicine and Surgery, 30*, 64–70.

Ikoma, A., Handwerker, H., Miyachi, Y., & Schmelz, M. (2005). Electrically evoked itch in humans. *Pain, 113*, 148–154.

Ikoma, A., Steinhoff, M., Ständer, S., Yosipovitch, G., & Schmelz, M. (2006). The neurobiology of itch. *Nature Reviews Neuroscience, 7*, 535–547.

Kaptchuk, T. J., Kelley, J. M., Conboy, L. A., Davis, R. B., Kerr, C. E., Jacobson, E. E., ... Lembo, A. J. (2008). Components of placebo effect: Randomised controlled trial in patients with irritable bowel syndrome. *BMJ (Clinical Research Ed.), 336*, 999–1003.

Katsuno, M., Aihara, M., Kojima, M., Osuna, H., Hosoi, J., Nakamura, M., ... Ikezawa, Z. (2003). Neuropeptides concentrations in the skin of a murine (NC/Nga mice) model of atopic dermatitis. *Journal of Dermatological Science, 33*, 55–65.

Kidd, B. L., & Urban, L. A. (2001). Mechanisms of inflammatory pain. *British Journal of Anaesthesia, 87*, 3–11.

Kim, H. S., & Yosipovitch, G. (2013). An aberrant parasympathetic response: A new perspective linking chronic stress and itch. *Experimental Dermatology, 22*, 239–244.

Kirsch, I. (1985). Response expectancy as a determinant of experience and behavior. *American Psychologist, 40*, 1189–1202.

Kirsch, I. (2000). Are drug and placebo effects in depression additive? *Biological Psychiatry, 47*, 733–735.

Klein, P. A., & Clark, R. A. (1999). An evidence-based review of the efficacy of antihistamines in relieving pruritus in atopic dermatitis. *Archives of Dermatology, 135*, 1522–1525.

Klinger, R. (2010). Das Potenzial des analgetischen Plazeboeffektes–S3–Leitlinien–Empfehlung zur Behandlung akuter und perioperativer Schmerzen [The potential of the analgesic placebo effect – S3 guideline recommendation on the clinical use for acute and perioperative pain]. *Anästhesiologie, Intensivmedizin, Notfallmedizin, Schmerztherapie, 45*, 22–29.

Klinger, R., Colloca, L., Bingel, U., & Flor, H. (2014). Placebo analgesia: Clinical applications. *Pain, 155*, 1055–1058. doi: 10.1016/j.pain.2013.12.007

Klinger, R., Soost, S., Flor, H., & Worm, M. (2007). Classical conditioning and expectancy in placebo hypoalgesia: A randomized controlled study in patients with atopic dermatitis and persons with healthy skin. *Pain, 128*, 31–39.

Klinger, R., Thomm, M., Bryant, M., & Becker, M. (2008). Patienteninformation und -aufklärung [Patient information and education]. In H. Laubenthal, M. Becker, S. Sauerland, & E. Neugebauer (Eds.), *Deutsche interdisziplinäre Vereinigung für Schmerztherapie (DIVS) S3-Leitlinie Behandlung akuter und perioperativer posttraumatischer* (pp. 19–22). Cologne, Germany: Deutscher Ärzte-Verlag.

Levine, J. D., & Gordon, N. C. (1984). Influence of the method of drug administration on analgesic response. *Nature, 312*, 755–756.

Levine, J. D., Gordon, N. C., & Fields, H. L. (1978). The mechanism of placebo analgesia. *Lancet, 312*, 654–657.

Liezmann, C., Klapp, B., & Peters, E. M. (2011). Stress, atopy and allergy: A re-evaluation from a psychoneuroimmunologic persepective. *Dermato-Endocrinology, 3*, 37–40.

McMahon, S. B., & Koltzenburg, M. (1992). Itching for an explanation. *Trends in Neurosciences, 15*, 497–501.

McRae, C. A., Prince, M. I., Hudson, M., Day, C. P., James, O. F. W., & Jones, D. E. J. (2003). Pain as a complication of use of opiate antagonists for symptom control in cholestasis. *Gastroenterology, 125*, 591–596.

Miller, F. G., & Colloca, L. (2011). The placebo phenomenon and medical ethics: Rethinking the relationship between informed consent and risk-benefit assessment. *Theoretical medicine and bioethics, 32*, 229–243.

Miller, F. G., Colloca, L., & Kaptchuk, T. J. (2009). The placebo effect: Illness and interpersonal healing. *Perspectives in Biology and Medicine, 52*, 518–539.

Mogil, J. S., Miermeister, F., Seifert, F., Strasburg, K., Zimmermann, K., Reinold, H., ... Reeh, P. W. (2005). Variable sensitivity to noxious heat is mediated by differential expression of the CGRP gene. *Proceedings of the National Academy of Sciences of the United States of America, 102*, 12938–12943.

Montgomery, G. H., & Kirsch, I. (1997). Classical conditioning and the placebo effect. *Pain, 72*, 107–113.

Narkus, A., Lehnigk, U., Häfner, D., Klinger, R., Pfaar, O. & Worm, M. (2013). The placebo effect in allergen-specific immunotherapy trials. *Clinical and Translational Allergy, 3*, 1–8.

Niemeier, V., Kupfer, J., & Gieler, U. (2000). Observations during itch-inducing lecture. *Dermatology and Psychosomatics / Dermatologie und Psychosomatik, 1*, 15–18. doi: 10.1159/000057993

Pacheco-López, G., Engler, H., Niemi, M.-B., & Schedlowski, M. (2006). Expectations and associations that heal: Immunomodulatory placebo effects and its neurobiology. *Brain, Behavior, and Immunity, 20*, 430–446.

Pavlovic, S., Daniltchenko, M., Tobin, D. J., Hagen, E., Hunt, S. P., Klapp, B. F., ... Peters, E. M. J. (2008). Further exploring the brain-skin connection: Stress worsens dermatitis via substance P-dependent neurogenic inflammation in mice. *The Journal of Investigative Dermatology, 128*, 434–446.

Phan, N. Q., Lotts, T., Antal, A., Bernhard, J. D., & Ständer, S. (2012). Systemic kappa opioid receptor agonists in the treatment of chronic pruritus: A literature review. *Acta Dermato-Venereologica, 92*, 555–560.

Pollo, A., Amanzio, M., Arslanian, A., Casadio, C., Maggi, G., & Benedetti, F. (2001). Response expectancies in placebo analgesia and their clinical relevance. *Pain, 93*, 77–84.

Price, D. D., & Fields, H. L. (1997). The contribution of desire and expectancy to placebo analgesia: Implications for new research strategies. In A. Harrington (Ed.), *The placebo effect: An interdiciplinary exploration* (pp. 117–137). Cambridge, MA: Harvard University Press.

Price, D. D., Finniss, D. G., & Benedetti, F. (2008). A comprehensive review of the placebo effect: Recent advances and current thought. *Annual Review of Psychology, 59*, 565–590.

Radziwill, K., & Kruszewski, J. (2011). Evaluation of the size of the placebo effect in treatments of allergic diseases and asthma based on a meta-analysis of efficacy trials of drugs. *Advances in Dermatology and Allergology, 28*, 372–377.

Savin, J. A. (1998). How should we define itching? *Journal of the American Academy of Dermatology, 39*, 268–269.

Schedlowski, M., & Pacheco-López, G. (2010). The learned immune response: Pavlov and beyond. *Brain, Behavior, and Immunity, 24*, 176–185.

Schmelz, M. (2002). Itch – mediators and mechanisms. *Journal of Dermatological Science, 28*, 91–96.

Schmelz, M. (2005). Itch and pain. *Dermatologic Therapy, 18*, 304–307.

Schmelz, M., Michael, K., Weidner, C., Schmidt, R., Torebjörk, H. E., & Handwerker, H. O. (2000). Which nerve fibers mediate the axon reflex flare in human skin? *Neuroreport, 11*, 645–648.

Schmelz, M., Schmidt, R., Bickel, A., Handwerker, H. O., & Torebjörk, H. E. (1997). Specific C-receptors for itch in human skin. *Journal of Neuroscience, 17*, 8003–8008.

Schmelz, M., Schmidt, R., Weidner, C., Hilliges, M., Torebjork, H. E., & Handwerker, H. O. (2003). Chemical response pattern of different classes of C-nociceptors to pruritogens and algogens. *Journal of Neurophysiology, 89*, 2441–2448.
Scholz, O. B., & Hermanns, N. (1994). Krankheitsverhalten und Kognitionen beeinflussen die Juckreiz-Wahrnehmung von Patienten mit atopischer Dermatitis [Illness behavior and cognitions influence the itching perception of patients with atopic dermatitis]. *Zeitschrift für klinische Psychologie, 23*, 127–135.
Siegel, S. (2002). Explanatory mechanisms for placebo effects: Pavlovian conditioning. In H. A. Guess, A. Kleinman, J. W. Kusek, & L. W. Engel (Eds.), *The science of the placebo: Toward an interdisciplinary research agenda* (pp. 133–157). London, UK: BMJ Books.
Singh, L. K., Pang, X., Alexacos, N., Letourneau, R., & Theoharides, T. C. (1999). Acute immobilization stress triggers skin mast cell degranulation via corticotropin releasing hormone, neurotensin, and substance P: A link to neurogenic skin disorders. *Brain, Behavior, and Immunity, 13*, 225–239.
Tey, H. L., & Yosipovitch, G. (2011). Targeted treatment of pruritus: A look into the future. *British Journal of Dermatology, 165*, 5–17.
Toyoda, M., Nakamura, M., Makino, T., Hino, T., Kagoura, M., & Morohashi, M. (2002). Nerve growth factor and substance P are useful plasma markers of disease activity in atopic dermatitis. *British Journal of Dermatology, 147*, 71–79.
Turner, J. A., Deyo, R. A., Loeser, J. D., Von Korff, M., & Fordyce, W. E. (1994). The importance of placebo effects in pain treatment and research. *Journal of the American Medical Association, 271*, 1609–1614.
Van Damme, S., Legrain, V., Vogt, J., & Crombez, G. (2010). Keeping pain in mind: A motivational account of attention to pain. *Neuroscience and Biobehavioral Reviews, 34*, 204–213.
Van Laarhoven, A. I. M., Kraaimaat, F. W., Wilder-Smith, O. H., & Evers, A. W. M. (2010). Role of attentional focus on bodily sensations in sensitivity to itch and pain. *Acta Dermato-Venereologica, 90*, 46–51.
Van Laarhoven, A. I. M., Vogelaar, M. L., Wilder-Smith, O. H., Van Riel, P. L. C. M., Van De Kerkhof, P. C. M., Kraaimaat, F. W., & Evers, A. W. M. (2011). Induction of nocebo and placebo effects on itch and pain by verbal suggestions. *Pain, 152*, 1486–1494.
Van Laarhoven, A. I. M., Walker, A. L., Wilder-Smith, O. H., Kroeze, S., van Riel, P. L. C. M., van de Kerkhof, P. C. M., . . . Evers, A. W. M. (2012). Role of induced negative and positive emotions in sensitivity to itch and pain in women. *British Journal of Dermatology, 167*, 262–269.
Vase, L., Riley, J. L., & Price, D. D. (2002). A comparison of placebo effects in clinical analgesic trials versus studies of placebo analgesia. *Pain, 99*, 443–452.
Vase, L., Robinson, M. E., Verne, G. N., & Price, D. D. (2003). The contributions of suggestion, desire, and expectation to placebo effects in irritable bowel syndrome patients. An empirical investigation. *Pain, 105*, 17–25.
Verhoeven, E. W. M., de Klerk, S., Kraaimaat, F. W., van de Kerkhof, P. C. M., de Jong, E. M. G. J., & Evers, A. W. M. (2008). Biopsychosocial mechanisms of chronic itch in patients with skin diseases: A review. *Acta Dermato-Venereologica, 88*, 211–218.
Verhoeven, E. W. M., Kraaimaat, F. W., de Jong, E. M. G. J., Schalkwijk, J., van de Kerkhof, P. C. M., & Evers, A. W. M. (2009). Effect of daily stressors on psoriasis: A prospective study. *Journal of Investigative Dermatology, 129*, 2075–2077.
Verhoeven, E. W. M., Kraaimaat, F. W., van de Kerkhof, P. C. M., van Weel, C., Duller, P., van der Valk, P. G. M., . . . Evers, A. W. M. (2007). Prevalence of physical symptoms of itch, pain and fatigue in patients with skin diseases in general practice. *British Journal of Dermatology, 156*, 1346–1349.
Voudouris, N. J., Peck, C. L., & Coleman, G. (1990). The role of conditioning and verbal expectancy in the placebo response. *Pain, 43*, 121–128.
Wahlgren, C. F. (1992). Pathophysiology of itching in urticaria and atopic dermatitis. *Allergy, 47*, 65–75.
Weisenberg, M., Raz, T., & Hener, T. (1998). The influence of film-induced mood on pain perception. *Pain, 76*, 365–375.
Weisshaar, E., & Dalgard, F. (2009). Epidemiology of itch: Adding to the burden of skin morbidity. *Acta Dermato-Venereologica, 89*, 339–350.
Wiech, K., & Tracey, I. (2009). The influence of negative emotions on pain: Behavioral effects and neural mechanisms. *NeuroImage, 47*, 987–994.
Yamaguchi, J., Aihara, M., Kobayashi, Y., Kambara, T., & Ikezawa, Z. (2009). Quantitative analysis of nerve growth factor (NGF) in the atopic dermatitis and psoriasis horny layer and effect of treatment on NGF in atopic dermatitis. *Journal of Dermatological Science, 53*, 48–54.
Yosipovitch, G., & Papoiu, A. D. P. (2008). What causes itch in atopic dermatitis? *Current Allergy and Asthma Reports, 8*, 306–311.
Zubieta, J. K., Bueller, J. A., Jackson, L. R., Scott, D. J., Xu, Y., Koeppe, R. A., . . . Stohler, C. S. (2005). Placebo effect mediated by endogenous opioid activity on mu-opioid receptors. *Journal of Neuroscience, 25*, 7754–7762.

Ariane Sölle

Department of Psychology
Outpatient Clinic of Behavior Therapy
University of Hamburg
Von-Melle-Park 5
20146 Hamburg
Germany
Tel. +49 40 42838-5374
Fax +49 40 42838-8008
E-mail ariane.soelle@uni-hamburg.de

Review Article

Learned Placebo Effects in the Immune System

Sabine Vits and Manfred Schedlowski

Institute of Medical Psychology and Behavioral Immunobiology, University Hospital Essen, University of Duisburg-Essen, Germany

Abstract. Associative learning processes are one of the major neuropsychological mechanisms steering the placebo response in different physiological systems and end organ functions. Learned placebo effects on immune functions are based on the bidirectional communication between the central nervous system (CNS) and the peripheral immune system. Based on this "hardware," experimental evidence in animals and humans showed that humoral and cellular immune functions can be affected by behavioral conditioning processes. We will first highlight and summarize data documenting the variety of experimental approaches conditioning protocols employed, affecting different immunological functions by associative learning. Taking a well-established paradigm employing a conditioned taste aversion model in rats with the immunosuppressive drug cyclosporine A (CsA) as an unconditioned stimulus (US) as an example, we will then summarize the efferent and afferent communication pathways as well as central processes activated during a learned immunosuppression. In addition, the potential clinical relevance of learned placebo effects on the outcome of immune-related diseases has been demonstrated in a number of different clinical conditions in rodents. More importantly, the learned immunosuppression is not restricted to experimental animals but can be also induced in humans. These data so far show that (i) behavioral conditioned immunosuppression is not limited to a single event but can be reproduced over time, (ii) immunosuppression cannot be induced by mere expectation, (iii) psychological and biological variables can be identified as predictors for this learned immunosuppression. Together with experimental approaches employing a placebo-controlled dose reduction these data provide a basis for new therapeutic approaches to the treatment of diseases where a suppression of immune functions is required via modulation of nervous system-immune system communication by learned placebo effects.

Keywords: neuropsychological mechanisms, placebo effect, learning, conditioning, immune functions

The Learned Immune Response

Learning and memory are fixed expressions in the immunological terminology describing recognition processes of antigens by T and B lymphocytes. In a less classical sense, immune responses can also be learned and memorized by associative learning or Pavlovian conditioning (Ader, 2003). Conditioning of immune functions commonly involves the pairing of an immunomodulatory compound such as an antigen or immunosuppressive drug (unconditioned stimulus, US) with a neutral (conditioned) stimulus (CS). Following several CS/US pairings, an association between the two stimuli is established, and the mere presentation of the CS induces immune responses closely mimicking the effect of the US (Ader, 2003; Schedlowski & Pacheco-López, 2010).

A prerequisite for behavioral conditioning of immune functions is the interaction between central nervous system (CNS) and the peripheral immune system. For a long time, the CNS and the immune system were thought to be independent systems each working on its own. However, within the last decades there is growing evidence that both systems share a common chemical language and are continuously exchanging information (Dantzer, O'Connor, Freund, Johnson, & Kelley, 2008; K. J. Tracey, 2010b). Indeed, it has been suggested that the immune system acts as a sensory organ with immune cells being mobile sentinels that inform the brain about the peripheral immune status (Blalock & Smith, 2007).

Within this framework, the learned immune response is not only a fascinating example of the bidirectional communication between the CNS and the immune system but can be conceived of as a learned placebo response that might offer possibilities for applications in the clinical setting as a supportive therapy to immunopharmacological regimens. In this review, the different approaches and paradigms in the field of conditioned immunomodulation will be summarized. In particular a well-established paradigm of learned immunosuppression in rodents and humans using Cyclosporine A (CsA) as an US will be highlighted. Subsequently, the therapeutic potential and possible applications of conditioned immunosuppression will be discussed.

Conditioned Immunomodulation – Different Approaches and Paradigms

A conditioned immune response was firstly demonstrated in guinea pigs by coworkers of Ivan Petrovic Pavlov, who reported a conditioned increase in peripheral leucocyte numbers after repeated injection of the plant extract Tapioka (US) together with a slight slit or heating of the skin (CS) (Metalnikov & Chorine, 1926). These early observations were later followed up and experimentally elaborated by Ader and Cohen (1975), who showed that the increase of antibody titers after injection of sheep erythrocytes was diminished not only in rats which received the immunosuppressant cyclophosphamide, but also in conditioned rats that were re-exposed to the CS (saccharine).

Since those pioneer studies, a large number of animal studies have shown that various immunological parameters can be affected by conditioning protocols. In these studies, typically a flavor or odor is employed as CS along with a pharmacological agent as US. The parameters affected comprise on humoral immune functions such as antibody responses (Alvarez-Borda, Ramirez-Amaya, Perez-Montfort, & Bermudez-Rattoni, 1995; Cohen, Ader, Green, & Bovbjerg, 1979) as well as cellular immune functions such as mitogen-induced lymphocyte proliferation (Lysle, Cunnick, Fowler, & Rabin, 1988), leucocyte numbers (S. Klosterhalfen & Klosterhalfen, 1987), the circulation of lymphocyte subpopulations (Husband, King, & Brown, 1987), the activity of natural killer cells (Ghanta, Hiramoto, Solvason, & Spector, 1985) or acute phase reactions (Exton, Bull, King, & Husband, 1995; Janz et al., 1996).

Several studies demonstrated that it is not only possible to suppress immune functions via conditioning protocols, but also to induce conditioned immune enhancement. A conditioned increase in natural killer cell activity has been shown in rodents (Solvason, Ghanta, & Hiramoto, 1988) as well as in healthy humans who received a sherbet sweet as a CS together with epinephrine injections (Buske-Kirschbaum, Kirschbaum, Stierle, Jabaij, & Hellhammer, 1994; Buske-Kirschbaum, Kirschbaum, Stierle, Lehnert, & Hellhammer, 1992). Furthermore, it was shown in rodents that the enhanced activity of cytotoxic T-lymphocytes through immunization can be conditioned by pairing the immunization procedure with camphor odor (Hiramoto et al., 1993). Another study showed that the immune activation in response to human recombinant interferon gamma can be conditioned in healthy subjects, using oral propylene glycol as conditioned stimulus (Longo et al., 1999).

Another line of research demonstrated that conditioning protocols can affect allergic reactions such as bronchial asthma and histamine release in guinea pigs (Justesen, Braun, Garrison, & Pendleton, 1970; Russell et al., 1984). In human studies, type 1 hypersensitivity reactions have been shown to be modulated by behavioral conditioning, measured by mast cell tryptase (Gauci, Husband, Saxarra, & King, 1994), nasal airflow, histamine release and subjective symptoms (Barrett, King, & Pang, 2000), and wheal size (Booth, Petrie, & Brook, 1995) (reviewed in Vits et al., 2011). One study that is particularly interesting with regard to its clinical relevance showed an antiallergic response in patients with house dust mite allergy who underwent a conditioning protocol with the antihistamine desloratadine as US (Goebel, Meykadeh, Kou, Schedlowski, & Hengge, 2008). While wheal sizes and subjective measures where influenced even in the absence of a distinct conditioned stimulus when desloratadine was replaced by a placebo pill (which points to an expectation-induced placebo response), a reduced basophil activation was only observed in the group who was re-exposed to a distinct conditioned stimulus (a novel tasting drink). This supports the assumption that unconscious immunological functions can be modulated by conditioning, whereas conscious processes can be modulated also by expectation (Benedetti et al., 2003).

Conditioned Taste Aversion and Immunosuppression – the CsA Paradigm

Cyclosporine A (CsA) is a calcineurin inhibitor which reduces the synthesis of TH_1-cytokines and is often employed in in clinical routine wherever a suppression of immune functions is required. A robust paradigm in rats was established with CsA as US and saccharine taste as a CS. When the two stimuli are repeatedly paired, two things occur: At the behavioral level, the rats avoid the saccharine solution drinking less of the saccharine solution. More importantly however, the re-exposure to the taste is inducing a learned immunosuppression. This paradigm has been repeatedly applied in rodents showing a conditioned reduction in spleen and thymus weight (Exton, von Hörsten, Voge, et al., 1998), reduced proliferation rates of spleen lymphocytes (Exton, von Hörsten, Schult, et al., 1998; Exton, von Hörsten, Voge, et al., 1998) and decreased interleukin-2 (IL-2) and g-interferon (g-IFN) concentrations (Exton, von Hörsten, Schult, et al., 1998; von Hörsten et al., 1998).

The CsA paradigm has also been successfully applied in humans (Albring et al., 2012; Goebel et al., 2002; Ober et al., 2012; Wirth et al., 2011). In these studies, healthy men receive CsA as US together with an unusual flavored and colored drink (CS). After several CS-US pairings, CsA was replaced by placebo capsules, which were now consumed together with the distinct CS. A learned immunosuppression after repeated re-exposure to the CS was demonstrated by reduced IL 2 and IFN-gamma levels as well as mRNA expression. The underlying pathways and biological mechanisms steering the learned placebo response on immune functions for this specific model have been elucidated in rodents.

Afferent Pathways

How does an immunopharmacological agent become an unconditioned stimulus? Either the drug itself directly acts on the brain or the CNS may "sense" the drug-induced immunological changes via two pathways: On the humoral way, the involved messengers such as cytokines or prostaglandins may either cross the blood brain barrier (Banks, 2005) or reach the brain via circumventricular organs (Goehler, Erisir, & Gaykema, 2006). The neural pathway on the other hand would require activation of neurons in the periphery that signal to the brain. The vagus nerve is well positioned to detect and inform the brain about

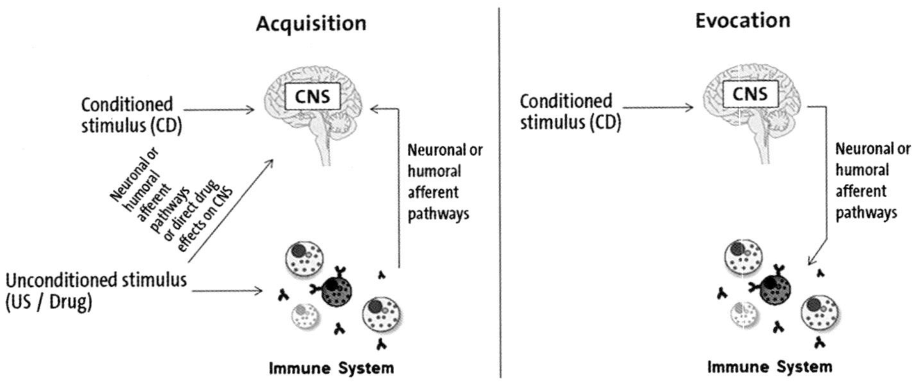

Figure 1. Principles of immunomodulation by behavioral conditioning. During acquisition, the unconditioned stimulus induces changes in the immune system. In addition, US information is signaled either indirectly to the CNS via messengers produced by the immune system (e.g., cytokines) or the US may act directly on the brain. Afferent pathways may be neuronal or humoral. The CNS subsequently integrates the peripheral information with the information of the conditioned stimulus given via sensory pathways. During evocation, presentation of the CS evokes activation of neuronal or humoral efferent pathways, inducing changes in the immune system that mimick the effect the US.

changes in the immune status (Tracey, 2002). It has been experimentally demonstrated that many effects in the CNS that are induced by changes in the immune system can be alleviated by prior vagotomy (Konsman, Luheshi, Bluthe, & Dantzer, 2000; Luheshi et al., 2000). Thus, it has been proposed that in CsA-induced conditioned immunosuppression, the vagus nerve may act as well as a major afferent route (Figure 1).

A recent study analyzed whether CsA is sensed via the chemosensitive vagus nerve or whether CsA directly acts on the brain. Data revealed that a single peripheral administration of CsA increases neuronal activity in the insular cortex and the amygdala as evident from increased electric activity, c-Fos expression and amygdaloid noradrenaline release. However, this increased neuronal activity was not affected by prior vagal deafferentation but rather seems to partially be induced by direct action of CsA on cortico-amygdaloid structures (Pacheco-López et al., 2013). Together, these data indicate that CsA as an unconditioned stimulus may directly act on the brain by a still unknown transduction mechanism.

Central Structures

The insular cortex and the amygdala as well as the ventromedial nucleus of the hypothalamus (VMH) are essential brain structures involved in conditioned immunosuppression (Pacheco-López et al., 2005). Confirming earlier observations, exitotoxic lesions showed that the insular cortex is necessary for both, acquisition and retrieval of the conditioned response (Bermudez-Rattoni & McGaugh, 1991; Cubero, Thiele, & Bernstein, 1999; Pacheco-López et al., 2005). In contrast, the amygdala only seems to mediate the input of visceral information necessary for acquisition, whereas the VMH appears to be involved only in the output pathway to the immune system.

Efferent Pathways

The sympathetic nervous system is one of the major pathways via which the CNS is communicating with the peripheral immune system in general. Specifically, this seems to be the major efferent pathway in the taste-immune learning paradigm, since the surgical denervation of the sympathetic nerve innervating the spleen blocked the conditioned reduction of cytokine production and lymphocyte proliferation (Exton, von Hörsten, Schult, et al., 1998). However, another study suggests that this is not the only efferent pathway for conditioned immunosuppressive effects as denervation of the splenic nerve still allows a conditioned reduction of ear swelling in contact hypersensitivity (Exton, Elfers, et al., 2000). Regarding involved transmitters and receptors, it was shown that noradrenaline is the predominant neurotransmitter mediating the learned immunosuppressive effects via beta-adrenoceptors (Exton et al., 2002). Recently it has been shown that this beta-adrenoceptor activation inhibits calcineurin activity in $CD4^+$ T-lymphocytes (Riether et al., 2011), demonstrating that both, the conditioned response and the pharmacological agent CsA are inducing immunosuppression via inhibition of calcineurin activity, however using different intracellular pathways.

Clinical Relevance of Learned Immunosuppressive Placebo Effect and Outlook

Behavioral conditioning of immune functions is not only an excellent model to study the bidirectional communication between the CNS and the peripheral immune system but also offers a new therapeutic approach that might allow to reduce the amount of medication required by supporting the therapeutic benefit through learned placebo effects.

Studies in rodents clearly document the therapeutic potential of conditioned immunosuppression, showing that the outcome of various diseases can be positively affected through learning protocols. The mortality rate and development of proteinuria in mice with lupus erythematosus were retarded in conditioned animals receiving a saccharine solution (CS) together with the immunosuppressive drug cyclophosphamide (US) (Ader & Cohen, 1982). Likewise, other studies showed that inflammatory processes can be reduced in rats with adjuvant arthritis (W. Klosterhalfen & Klosterhalfen, 1983), skin and heart allograft survival prolonged (Exton, Schult, et al., 1998; Gorczynski, 1990; Grochowicz et al., 1991) and tumor growth can be delayed (Ghanta, Hiramoto, Solvason, Soong, & Hiramoto, 1990; Ghanta, Hiramoto, Solvason, & Spector, 1987; Ghanta, Miura, Hiramoto, & Hiramoto, 1988) by using conditioning procedures. A therapeutic approach using a conditioning protocol has been tested in patients with multiple sclerosis. In this study, patients who received their treatment with cyclophosphamide together with a conditioned stimulus showed a decrease in peripheral leukocyte counts when re-exposed to the CS together with a subtherapeutic dose of cyclophosphamide (Giang et al., 1996).

A prerequisite for applying learning protocols in a clinical setting is the reproducibility of learned immunosuppressive effects over time. This has been recently documented in rodents as well as humans (Exton, von Hörsten, et al., 2000; Wirth et al., 2011). Regarding the recall of the learned immunosuppression, one study in healthy participants showed that the effect is not present after one re-exposure to the conditioned stimulus, but after four re-exposures (Albring et al., 2012). This is in line with an earlier study in rats that proposed that the engram is strengthened with repeated re-exposures to the CS (Niemi et al., 2007).

Many placebo responses in clinical conditions such as pain or Parkinson disease have been shown to be influenced by verbal instructions that manipulate the expectation of the participant or patient related to treatment efficacy (Bingel et al., 2011; Lidstone et al., 2010; I. Tracey, 2010a). Within the framework of conditioned immunosuppression as a learned placebo response, an interesting question is whether immunosuppression can be induced by mere expectation of the participants as well. Recently, this was investigated within the CsA paradigm showing that expectation alone does not induce an immunosuppression (Albring et al., 2012), confirming earlier observations which proposed that neuroendocrine and immunological functions can be affected by learning processes but not via cognitive factors such as expectation (Benedetti et al., 2003).

When thinking about employing conditioning protocols in clinical routine, the goal will be to employ conditioning procedures to support pharmacological therapies rather than to replace it. Placebo-controlled dose reduction (PCDR), in which a certain amount of the usual dose of a drug is replaced by a placebo is a concept that might maintain the efficacy of a treatment while reducing the dose of medication and unwanted side effects (Doering & Rief, 2012). In one study, the partial replacement (25% or 50%) of corticosteroids with a placebo in patients with psoriasis, induced a similar symptom reduction compared to a full dose treatment (Ader et al., 2010). A placebo controlled dose reduction was also tested in children with attention-deficit hyperactivity disorder (ADHD; Sandler, Glesne, & Bodfish, 2010) and cough (Leech, Mazzone, & Farrell, 2012).

Instead of employing partial reinforcement protocols, another possibility is to continuously reinforce the conditioned response by presenting the CS together with subtherapeutic doses of the US. The effectiveness of this concept was demonstrated in heart allograft model in rats. Those rats that were given subtherapeutic doses of CsA together with the CS during evocation, showed a significant longer survival time compared to the control groups (Exton et al., 1999). Putting these findings into learning theory, this synergistic effect may be attributable to a reconsolidation process, with a reconsolidation of the memory trace (immunosuppression) when it is activated via re-exposure to the CS. The consistent "reminder" by the otherwise ineffective subtherapeutic dose of CsA might have strengthened the engram and counteracted the extinction processes of learned immunosuppression. This hypothesis remains to be tested in future sophisticated experimental studies.

Another important aspect within the framework of placebo responses in general is the question, who will respond to a "placebo therapy" and are there predictors of placebo responses (Kaptchuk et al., 2008). These predictors might be stable features such as personality traits, genetic or other physiological factors or situational factors included in an experimental of clinical setting. With identifying stable predictors within persons, that is, distinguishing between "placebo responders" and "placebo non-responders," quick decisions which person would benefit from a commensurate therapy could be made. Evidence for such predictors to distinguish between "placebo responders" and "placebo non-responders" is scarce, but some variables have been identified. In the case of conditioned immunosuppression, recent evidence shows that state anxiety as well as plasma noradrenaline together with IL-2 concentrations at baseline predicted almost 60% of the variance in the conditioned response, measured by suppressed IL-2 levels (Ober et al., 2012).

The applicability and effectiveness of employing conditioning procedures together with immunopharmacological regimen across various immune-related diseases are not thoroughly investigated yet. However, there is a growing body of evidence that the learned immunosuppression offers great potential for therapeutic applications that could maximize the patient's benefit by minimizing unwanted aspects of the treatment such as intensive medication costs or unwanted drug side effects.

References

Ader, R. (2003). Conditioned immunomodulation: research needs and directions. *Brain, Behavior, and Immunity, 17*, S51–S57.

Ader, R., & Cohen, N. (1975). Behaviorally conditioned immunosuppression. *Psychosomatic Medicine, 37*, 333–340.

Ader, R., & Cohen, N. (1982). Behaviorally conditioned immunosuppression and murine systemic lupus erythematosus. *Science, 215*, 1534–1536.

Ader, R., Mercurio, M. G., Walton, J., James, D., Davis, M., Ojha, V., . . . Fiorentino, D. (2010). Conditioned pharmacotherapeutic effects: A preliminary study. *Psychosomatic Medicine, 72*, 192–197. doi: 10.1097/PSY.0b013e3181cbd38b

Albring, A., Wendt, L., Benson, S., Witzke, O., Kribben, A., Engler, H., & Schedlowski, M. (2012). Placebo effects on the immune response in humans: The role of learning and expectation. *PLoS One, 7*, e49477. doi: 10.1371/journal.pone.0049477

Alvarez-Borda, B., Ramirez-Amaya, V., Perez-Montfort, R., & Bermudez-Rattoni, F. (1995). Enhancement of antibody production by a learning paradigm. *Neurobiology of Learning and Memory, 64*, 103–105.

Banks, W. A. (2005). Blood-brain barrier transport of cytokines: A mechanism for neuropathology. *Current Pharmaceutical Design, 11*, 973–984.

Barrett, J. E., King, M. G., & Pang, G. (2000). Conditioning rhinitis in allergic humans. *Annals of the New York Academy of Sciences, 917*, 853–859.

Benedetti, F., Pollo, A., Lopiano, L., Lanotte, M., Vighetti, S., & Rainero, I. (2003). Conscious expectation and unconscious conditioning in analgesic, motor, and hormonal placebo/nocebo responses. *Journal of Neuroscience, 23*, 4315–4323.

Bermudez-Rattoni, F., & McGaugh, J. L. (1991). Insular cortex and amygdala lesions differentially affect acquisition on inhibitory avoidance and conditioned taste aversion. *Brain Research, 549*, 165–170.

Bingel, U., Wanigasekera, V., Wiech, K., Ni Mhuircheartaigh, R., Lee, M. C., Ploner, M., & Tracey, I. (2011). The effect of treatment expectation on drug efficacy: Imaging the analgesic benefit of the opioid remifentanil. *Science Translational Medicine, 3*, 70ra14. doi: 10.1126/scitranslmed.3001244

Blalock, J. E., & Smith, E. M. (2007). Conceptual development of the immune system as a sixth sense. *Brain, Behavior, and Immunity, 21*, 23–33.

Booth, R. J., Petrie, K. J., & Brook, R. J. (1995). Conditioning allergic skin responses in humans: A controlled trial. *Psychosomatic Medicine, 57*, 492–495.

Buske-Kirschbaum, A., Kirschbaum, C., Stierle, H., Jabaij, L., & Hellhammer, D. (1994). Conditioned manipulation of natural killer (NK) cells in humans using a discriminative learning protocol. *Biological Psychology, 38*, 143–155.

Buske-Kirschbaum, A., Kirschbaum, C., Stierle, H., Lehnert, H., & Hellhammer, D. (1992). Conditioned increase of natural killer cell activity (NKCA) in humans. *Psychosomatic Medicine, 54*, 123–132.

Cohen, N., Ader, R., Green, N., & Bovbjerg, D. (1979). Conditioned suppression of a thymus-independent antibody response. *Psychosomatic Medicine, 41*, 487–491.

Cubero, I., Thiele, T. E., & Bernstein, I. L. (1999). Insular cortex lesions and taste aversion learning: Effects of conditioning method and timing of lesion. *Brain Research, 839*, 323–330.

Dantzer, R., O'Connor, J. C., Freund, G. G., Johnson, R. W., & Kelley, K. W. (2008). From inflammation to sickness and depression: When the immune system subjugates the brain. *Nature Reviews Neuroscience, 9*, 46–56.

Doering, B. K., & Rief, W. (2012). Utilizing placebo mechanisms for dose reduction in pharmacotherapy. *Trends in Pharmacological Sciences, 33*, 165–172. doi: 10.1016/j.tips.2011.12.001

Exton, M. S., Bull, D. F., King, M. G., & Husband, A. J. (1995). Modification of body temperature and sleep state using behavioral conditioning. *Physiology & Behavior, 57*, 723–729.

Exton, M. S., Elfers, A., Jeong, W. Y., Bull, D. F., Westermann, J., & Schedlowski, M. (2000). Conditioned suppression of contact sensitivity is independent of sympathetic splenic innervation. *American Journal of Physiology – Regulatory, Integrative and Comparative Physiology, 279*, R1310–R1315.

Exton, M. S., Gierse, C., Meier, B., Mosen, M., Xie, Y., Frede, S., . . . Schedlowski, M. (2002). Behaviorally conditioned immunosuppression in the rat is regulated via noradrenaline and beta-adrenoceptors. *Journal of Neuroimmunology, 131*, 21–30.

Exton, M. S., Schult, M., Donath, S., Strubel, T., Bode, U., del Rey, A., . . . Schedlowski, M. (1999). Conditioned immunosuppression makes subtherapeutic cyclosporin effective via splenic innervation. *American Journal of Physiology, 276*, R1710–R1717.

Exton, M. S., Schult, M., Donath, S., Strubel, T., Nagel, E., Westermann, J., & Schedlowski, M. (1998). Behavioral conditioning prolongs heart allograft survival in rats. *Transplantation Proceedings, 30*, 2033.

Exton, M. S., von Hörsten, S., Schult, M., Vöge, J., Strubel, T., Donath, S., . . . Schedlowski, M. (1998). Behaviorally conditioned immunosuppression using cyclosporine A: Central nervous system reduces IL-2 production via splenic innervation. *Journal of Neuroimmunology, 88*, 182–191.

Exton, M. S., von Hörsten, S., Strubel, T., Donath, S., Schedlowski, M., & Westermann, J. (2000). Conditioned alterations of specific blood leukocyte subsets are reconditionable. *Neuroimmunomodulation, 7*, 106–114.

Exton, M. S., Von Hörsten, S., Vöge, J., Westermann, J., Schult, M., Nagel, E., & Schedlowski, M. (1998). Conditioned taste aversion produced by cyclosporine A: Concomitant reduction in lymphoid organ weight and splenocyte proliferation. *Physiology & Behavior, 63*, 241–247.

Gauci, M., Husband, A. J., Saxarra, H., & King, M. G. (1994). Pavlovian conditioning of nasal tryptase release in human subjects with allergic rhinitis. *Physiology & Behavior, 55*, 823–825.

Ghanta, V., Hiramoto, R. N., Solvason, B., & Spector, N. H. (1987). Influence of conditioned natural immunity on tumor growth. *Annals of the New York Academy of Sciences, 496*, 637–646.

Ghanta, V. K., Hiramoto, N. S., Solvason, H. B., Soong, S. J., & Hiramoto, R. N. (1990). Conditioning: A new approach to immunotherapy. *Cancer Research, 50*, 4295–4299.

Ghanta, V. K., Hiramoto, R. N., Solvason, H. B., & Spector, N. H. (1985). Neural and environmental influences on neoplasia and conditioning of NK activity. *Journal of Immunology, 135*, 848s–852s.

Ghanta, V. K., Miura, T., Hiramoto, N. S., & Hiramoto, R. N. (1988). Augmentation of natural immunity and regulation of tumor growth by conditioning. *Annals of the New York Academy of Sciences, 521*, 29–42.

Giang, D. W., Goodman, A. D., Schiffer, R. B., Mattson, D. H., Petrie, M., Cohen, N., & Ader, N. (1996). Conditioning of cyclophosphamide-induced leukopenia in humans. *Journal of Neuropsychiatry and Clinical Neurosciences, 8*, 194–201.

Goebel, M. U., Meykadeh, N., Kou, W., Schedlowski, M., & Hengge, U. R. (2008). Behavioral conditioning of antihistamine effects in patients with allergic rhinitis. *Psychotherapy and Psychosomatics, 77*, 227–234.

Goebel, M. U., Trebst, A. E., Steiner, J., Xie, Y. F., Exton, M. S., Frede, S., . . . Schedlowski, M. (2002). Behavioral conditioning of immunosuppression is possible in humans. *FASEB Journal, 16*, 1869–1873.

Goehler, L. E., Erisir, A., & Gaykema, R. P. (2006). Neural-immune interface in the rat area postrema. *Neuroscience, 140*, 1415–1434.

Gorczynski, R. M. (1990). Conditioned enhancement of skin allografts in mice. *Brain, Behavior, and Immunity, 4*, 85–92.

Grochowicz, P. M., Schedlowski, M., Husband, A. J., King, M. G., Hibberd, A. D., & Bowen, K. M. (1991). Behavioral conditioning prolongs heart allograft survival in rats. *Brain, Behavior, and Immunity, 5*, 349–356.

Hiramoto, R. N., Hsueh, C. M., Rogers, C. F., Demissie, S., Hiramoto, N. S., Soong, S. J., & Ghanta, V. K. (1993). Conditioning of the allogeneic cytotoxic lymphocyte response. *Pharmacology Biochemistry and Behavior, 44*, 275–280. doi: 10.1016/0091-3057(93)90462-3

Husband, A. J., King, M. G., & Brown, R. (1987). Behaviourally conditioned modification of T cell subset ratios in rats. *Immunology Letters, 14*, 91–94.

Janz, L. J., Green-Johnson, J., Murray, L., Vriend, C. Y., Nance, D. M., Greenberg, A. H., & Dyck, D. G. (1996). Pavlovian conditioning of LPS-induced responses: effects on corticosterone, splenic NE, and IL-2 production. *Physiology & Behavior, 59*, 1103–1109.

Justesen, D. R., Braun, E. W., Garrison, R. G., & Pendleton, R. B. (1970). Pharmacological differentiation of allergic and classically conditioned asthma in the guinea pig. *Science, 170*, 864–866.

Kaptchuk, T. J., Kelley, J. M., Deykin, A., Wayne, P. M., Lasagna, L. C., Epstein, I. O., ... Wechsler, M. E. (2008). Do "placebo responders" exist? *Contemporary Clinical Trials, 29*, 587–595. doi: 10.1016/j.cct.2008.02.002

Klosterhalfen, S., & Klosterhalfen, W. (1987). Classically conditioned effects of cyclophosphamide on white blood cell counts in rats. *Annals of the New York Academy of Sciences, 496*, 569–577.

Klosterhalfen, W., & Klosterhalfen, S. (1983). Pavlovian conditioning of immunosuppression modifies adjuvant arthritis in rats. *Behavioral Neuroscience, 97*, 663–666.

Konsman, J. P., Luheshi, G. N., Bluthe, R. M., & Dantzer, R. (2000). The vagus nerve mediates behavioural depression, but not fever, in response to peripheral immune signals; a functional anatomical analysis. *European Journal of Neuroscience, 12*, 4434–4446.

Leech, J., Mazzone, S. B., & Farrell, M. J. (2012). The effect of placebo conditioning on capsaicin-evoked urge to cough. *Chest, 142*, 951–957.

Lidstone, S. C., Schulzer, M., Dinelle, K., Mak, E., Sossi, V., Ruth, T. J., ... Stoessl, A. J. (2010). Effects of expectation on placebo-induced dopamine release in Parkinson disease. *Archives of General Psychiatry, 67*, 857–865. doi: 10.1001/archgenpsychiatry.2010.88

Longo, D. L., Duffey, P. L., Kopp, W. C., Heyes, M. P., Alvord, W. G., Sharfman, W. H., ... Rosenstein, D. L. (1999). Conditioned immune response to interferon-gamma in humans. *Clinical Immunology, 90*, 173–181.

Luheshi, G. N., Bluthe, R. M., Rushforth, D., Mulcahy, N., Konsman, J. P., Goldbach, M., & Dantzer, R. (2000). Vagotomy attenuates the behavioural but not the pyrogenic effects of interleukin-1 in rats. *Autonomic Neuroscience, 85*, 127–132.

Lysle, D. T., Cunnick, J. E., Fowler, H., & Rabin, B. S. (1988). Pavlovian conditioning of shock-induced suppression of lymphocyte reactivity: Acquisition, extinction, and preexposure effects. *Life Sciences, 42*, 2185–2194.

Metalnikov, S., & Chorine, V. (1926). The role of conditioned reflexes in immunity. In S. Locke, R. Ader, H. Besedovsky, & N. Hall (Eds.), *Foundations of psychoneuroimmunology* (pp. 263–267). New York, NY: Aldine.

Niemi, M. B., Harting, M., Kou, W., Del Rey, A., Besedovsky, H. O., Schedlowski, M., & Pacheco-López, G. (2007). Taste-immunosuppression engram: Reinforcement and extinction. *Journal of Neuroimmunology, 188*, 74–79.

Ober, K., Benson, S., Vogelsang, M., Bylica, A., Gunther, D., Witzke, O., ... Schedlowski, M. (2012). Plasma noradrenaline and state anxiety levels predict placebo response in learned immunosuppression. *Clinical Pharmacology & Therapeutics, 91*, 220–226. doi: 10.1038/clpt.2011.214

Pacheco-López, G., Doenlen, R., Krügel, U., Arnold, M., Wirth, T., Riether, C., ... Schedlowski, M. (2013). Neurobehavioural activation during peripheral immunosuppression. *International Journal of Neuropsychopharmacology, 16*(1), 137–149.

Pacheco-López, G., Niemi, M. B., Kou, W., Harting, M., Fandrey, J., & Schedlowski, M. (2005). Neural substrates for behaviorally conditioned immunosuppression in the rat. *Journal of Neuroscience, 25*, 2330–2337.

Riether, C., Kavelaars, A., Wirth, T., Pacheco-López, G., Doenlen, R., Willemen, H., ... Engler, H. (2011). Stimulation of beta(2)-adrenergic receptors inhibits calcineurin activity in CD4(+) T cells via PKA-AKAP interaction. *Brain, Behavior, and Immunity, 25*, 59–66. doi: 10.1016/j.bbi.2010.07.248

Russell, M., Dark, K. A., Cummins, R. W., Ellman, G., Callaway, E., & Peeke, H. V. (1984). Learned histamine release. *Science, 225*, 733–734.

Sandler, A. D., Glesne, C. E., & Bodfish, J. W. (2010). Conditioned placebo dose reduction: A new treatment in attention-deficit hyperactivity disorder? *Journal of Developmental & Behavioral Pediatrics, 31*, 369–375.

Schedlowski, M., & Pacheco-López, G. (2010). The learned immune response: Pavlov and beyond. *Brain, Behavior, and Immunity, 24*, 176–185.

Solvason, H. B., Ghanta, V. K., & Hiramoto, R. N. (1988). Conditioned augmentation of natural killer cell activity: Independence from nociceptive effects and dependence on interferon-beta. *Journal of Immunology, 140*, 661–665.

Tracey, I. (2010a). Getting the pain you expect: Mechanisms of placebo, nocebo and reappraisal effects in humans. *Nature Medicine, 16*, 1277–1283.

Tracey, K. J. (2002). The inflammatory reflex. *Nature, 420*, 853–859.

Tracey, K. J. (2010b). Understanding immunity requires more than immunology. *Nature Immunology, 11*, 561–564.

Vits, S., Cesko, E., Enck, P., Hillen, U., Schadendorf, D., & Schedlowski, M. (2011). Behavioural conditioning as the mediator of placebo responses in the immune system. *Philosophical Transactions of the Royal Society B Biological Sciences, 366*, 1799–1807.

von Hörsten, S., Exton, M. S., Schult, M., Nagel, E., Stalp, M., Schweitzer, G., ... Westermann, J. (1998). Behaviorally conditioned effects of Cyclosporine A on the immune system of rats: specific alterations of blood leukocyte numbers and decrease of granulocyte function. *Journal of Neuroimmunology, 85*, 193–201.

Wirth, T., Ober, K., Prager, G., Vogelsang, M., Benson, S., Witzke, O., ... Schedlowski, M. (2011). Repeated recall of learned immunosuppression: Evidence from rats and men. *Brain, Behavior, and Immunity, 25*, 1444–1451.

Sabine Vits

Institute of Medical Psychology and Behavioral Immunobiology
University Hospital Essen
University of Duisburg-Essen
Hufelandstr. 55
45122 Essen
Germany
Tel. +49 201 723-4505
Fax +49 201 723-5948
E-mail sabine.vits@uk-essen.de

The Effects of Manipulating Verbal Suggestions on Physical Performance

Elisa Carlino, Fabrizio Benedetti, and Antonella Pollo

Department of Neuroscience, University of Turin Medical School, and National Institute of Neuroscience, Turin, Italy

Abstract. Expectation induced by verbal suggestions is known to be a central mechanism in the generation of the placebo response in different physiological and pathological conditions. Here, we analyze the impact of different verbal suggestions in an experimental setting, measuring work performed, and rate of perceived exertion in healthy subjects undergoing strenuous exercise. A double protocol is used, with different probabilities of receiving what is believed to be an ergogenic substance (in fact, a placebo), with or without an associated conditioning procedure. We show that while high verbal suggestions of motor improvement can work alone, low verbal suggestions produce a response only after conditioning, and that in the absence of verbal suggestions (open-label placebo) no response can ever be elicited. These results can be useful for the design of both clinical trial and sports training protocols.

Keywords: placebo, expectation, conditioning, quadriceps, human

The placebo response, that is, the effect following the administration of an inert pharmacological or procedural treatment, has been widely investigated in medicine, where its neurobiological mechanisms are being unraveled in pathological conditions such as pain, motor system dysfunctions, depression, as well as in the intact immune and endocrine systems (Benedetti, 2008; Pollo, Carlino, & Benedetti, 2011). The main mechanisms involved appear to be unconscious Pavlovian conditioning and cognitive expectations, whereby the subject anticipates the treatment outcome (Lui et al., 2010; Price, Finniss, & Benedetti, 2008). The placebo treatment, along with the whole psychosocial context surrounding the therapeutic act, exerts a powerful effect on the nervous system, modulating neuronal activity and triggering the release of endogenous substances acting on specific targets (e.g., opioids and cannabinoids for placebo analgesia or dopamine in the case of Parkinson's disease; Amanzio & Benedetti, 1999; Benedetti, Amanzio, Rosato, & Blanchard, 2011; de la Fuente-Fernandez et al., 2001; Petrovic, Kalso, Petersson, & Ingvar, 2002; Zubieta et al., 2005).

Expectations can be raised in several ways, one of the most powerful being verbal suggestions (Bingel et al., 2011). Attempts have been made to evaluate the impact of differing verbal suggestions, with particular regard to the outcome certainty induced in the subject. For example, thoracic surgery patients in the post-operative phase requested less analgesic treatment than controls when they (mistakenly) believed a basal intravenous infusion contained an analgesic drug, and this effect was greater when they were deceived altogether than when they were told they had a 50% chance of receiving the basal analgesic (Pollo et al., 2001). In the experimental setting, subjects reacted with greater changes in heart rate and alertness after a sham caffeine dose given deceptively (certain expectations) rather than in a double-blind protocol (uncertain expectations) (Kirsch & Weixel, 1988). At the neurochemical level, it was shown that in Parkinson's disease patients dopamine release in the ventral striatum (associated with the placebo response) was modulated by the strength of expectation (Lidstone et al., 2010). Although the grading of expectations is starting to be addressed (Elsenbruch et al., 2012), investigations specifically analyzing the impact of outcome certainty on the placebo response are needed.

Placebo responses are not confined to the clinical domain. For example, they have also been studied in physical performance (Beedie & Foad, 2009), where the administration of sham ergogenic supplements or procedures induced improvements of muscle work and decrease of muscle fatigue perception (Pollo, Carlino, & Benedetti, 2008). Interestingly, negative expectations induced opposite effects, that is, nocebo responses (Beedie, Coleman, & Foad, 2007; Pollo, Carlino, Vase, & Benedetti, 2012). In the sport field, placebo responses have relevance for their possible exploitation in training paradigms, but at the same time they fuel ethical debate because of their potential use in doping, alongside illicit drugs (Benedetti, Pollo, & Colloca, 2007). Moreover, the physiological context of exercise offers greater protocol flexibility compared to the clinical setting, where ethical constraints limit the demands that can be imposed on patients. Therefore, we

DOI: 10.1027/2151-2604/a000178

addressed the following questions in an experimental setting, by employing a protocol measuring work and fatigue in healthy subjects undergoing strenuous exercise: (1) whether the degree of certainty affects the placebo response produced by the administration of a sham caffeine drink used as an ergogenic placebo; (2) whether the placebo response is influenced in a different way when verbal suggestions are given only or they are reinforced by a conditioning procedure. In this work we used two experimental groups from our previous paper (Pollo et al., 2008).

Methods

Subjects

A total of 110 healthy male volunteers recruited from the student population of the University of Turin participated in the study after signing a written informed consent form in which the experimental procedure was described in detail. Female subjects were excluded a priori in order to avoid possible gender differences. All subjects engaged in recreational fitness training and were asked to avoid hard exercise starting from at least 24 hr before the experimental sessions. They were either nonsmokers or light smokers (< 10 cigarettes/day). During the first visit, their medical history was recorded in order to rule out main diseases, and an electrocardiogram was performed to assess their heart response to exercise. The subjects were randomly subdivided into ten groups, whose characteristics are summarized in Table 1. All the subjects were asked to refrain from consuming caffeine-containing beverages for 48 hr before each experimental session, as well as alcohol and any drug. All the experimental sessions were conducted in the morning at approximately the same time for each subject, after a standardized light breakfast had been consumed. This consisted of a cup of milk or fruit juice and a muffin or biscuits, whose energy content was about 2,000 kJ. Twelve subjects followed their habit of not having any breakfast. Dietary adherence was assessed by means of a brief oral questionnaire before the start of each session. All the experimental procedures were conducted in conformance with the policies and principles contained in the Declaration of Helsinki.

Placebo Caffeine as an Ergogenic Agent

During the study, only placebo doses of caffeine were administered (< 1% of the dose needed to affect performance). However, dietary caffeine intake was assessed to ascertain the subjects' willingness to assume caffeine-containing beverages during the experiments. The subjects always received 20 mL of decaffeinated coffee (with or without a noncaloric sweetener) along with different expectations (see Experimental Groups). The caffeine residual content of the decaffeinated coffee (Lavazza Dek, Turin, Italy) was $\leq 0.1\%$ in accordance with European Community rules. This corresponds to a content of about 2–4 mg per cup, largely below the doses used to assess caffeine influence on muscular performance, which amounts to about 420 mg in a subject weighing 70 kg (Kalmar & Cafarelli, 1999). Therefore, the caffeine dose we used corresponded to about 0.5–1% of the dose necessary to improve performance (what can be called "placebo caffeine").

Experimental Groups

In a previous work we investigated the placebo effect on motor performance after the deceptive administration of sham caffeine (Pollo et al., 2008). The control subjects were informed that they belonged to the control group for a study on the effects of caffeine on muscular performance. Conversely, the placebo subjects (P) were deceived, as they were told that they belonged to the group testing the effect of caffeine: In this way, certainty about performance increase was maximized. In order to assess the effect of varying levels of certainty, these two groups are reanalyzed here and labeled as the NT (no treatment) and $CAFF_{100\%}$ groups, together with three more groups with different specific probabilities of motor improvement (see Figure 1). In the 50% group ($CAFF_{50\%}$), the subjects had to choose between two cups of decaffeinated coffee, labeled with the letters A and B, and they were told that only one cup contained the high dose of coffee, whereas the other was a decaffeinated beverage. Accordingly, they were informed that they had a 50% chance of motor improvement. Subjects of the 50% group always received the following instruction "You have to choose one of these two cups: One of them contains the high dose of coffee, whereas the other is a decaffeinated beverage. You have a 50% chance of motor improvement." In the 25% group ($CAFF_{25\%}$), the subjects were presented with four different cups of decaffeinated coffee labeled with four different letters (A, B, C, and D) and they were told that only one cup contained the high dose of coffee, whereas the others were decaffeinated drinks. Accordingly, they were informed to have a 25% chance of motor improvement. Subjects of the 25% group always received the following instruction "You have to choose one of these four cups: One of them contains the high dose of coffee, whereas the others are decaffeinated beverages. You have a 25% chance of motor improvement." The 0% group ($CAFF_{0\%}$) received only one cup, together with the information that it contained a decaffeinated drink, and accordingly did not have any expectation of improvement. Subjects of the 0% group always received the following instruction "You are receiving a decaffeinated drink because this is a control session." This last group was introduced as a further control, in which the ritual of drinking was maintained (as for the told caffeine-get placebo groups) but without expectations of motor improvement (as for the control group).

Experimental Design

Physical performance was performed by using a leg extensor device (Technogym, Italy), which involves the

Table 1. Subject characteristics

Protocol 1 (verbal suggestions only)					
Group	NT_1	$CAFF_{1\text{-}100\%}$	$CAFF_{1\text{-}50\%}$	$CAFF_{1\text{-}25\%}$	$CAFF_{1\text{-}0\%}$
Number of subjects	11	11	11	11	11
Age (years)	21.45 ± 1.51	21.64 ± 2.73	20.18 ± 1.40	21.00 ± 1.18	20.55 ± 1.21
Weight (kg)	71 ± 9.41	72.64 ± 8.57	68.64 ± 8.36	75.91 ± 13.54	71.82 ± 8.01
Height (m)	1.78 ± 0.06	1.79 ± 0.09	55.45 ± 0.04	55.91 ± 0.05	57.73 ± 1.79
RM-1 (kg)	45.45 ± 12.93	55 ± 12.45	55.45 ± 7.57	55.91 ± 11.14	57.73 ± 8.76
Weight lifted (kg)	27.27 ± 7.76	33 ± 7.47	33.27 ± 4.54	33.55 ± 6.68	34.64 ± 5.26
BMI (kg/m^2)	22.51 ± 2.93	22.61 ± 2.40	22.49 ± 2.79	24.34 ± 4.88	20.36 ± 6.79
Protocol 2 (verbal suggestions + conditioning)					
Group	NT_2	$CAFF_{2\text{-}100\%}$	$CAFF_{2\text{-}50\%}$	$CAFF_{2\text{-}25\%}$	$CAFF_{2\text{-}0\%}$
Number of subjects	11	11	11	11	11
Age (years)	22.36 ± 3.07	21.36 ± 1.75	20.82 ± 1.60	20.64 ± 0.81	21.00 ± 1.79
Weight (kg)	70 ± 8.12	70.36 ± 12.61	70.27 ± 5.26	72.09 ± 10.75	74.23 ± 12.40
Height (m)	1.77 ± 0.06	1.79 ± 0.06	54.55 ± 0.03	51.82 ± 0.22	59.55 ± 0.07
RM-1 (kg)	57.27 ± 13.85	60.45 ± 11.72	54.55 ± 7.89	51.82 ± 13.47	59.55 ± 10.36
Weight lifted (kg)	34.36 ± 8.31	36.27 ± 7.03	32.73 ± 4.73	31.18 ± 8.22	36.00 ± 6.12
BMI (kg/m^2)	22.42 ± 2.33	22.06 ± 3.90	22.27 ± 2.05	25.97 ± 10.83	22.95 ± 3.33

Note: BMI = Body mass index (weight/height^2).

quadriceps muscles only (Pollo et al., 2008, 2012). In this way, we avoided the involvement of many muscles, which might confound the interpretation of the results. After familiarization with the experimental set up on their first visit to the lab, all subjects underwent the determination of the 1-repetition maximum (1-RM), that is, the maximum weight that could be lifted once. In fact, the subjects performed a single extension with 5 kg increments, starting at 15 kg, until unable to complete the task. The last successfully lifted weight was noted as the 1-RM and the subject subsequently rested for 30 min. Before each session, blood pressure was measured at the left arm by means of a standard sphygmomanometer and stethoscope. The electrocardiogram was continuously monitored to check for ectopic beats and/or excessive increase in heart rate, signaling the need of exercise interruption. In no case was it necessary to interrupt the experiment.

After the 30-min rest, the subjects performed the leg extension exercise to voluntary fatigue, until complete exhaustion. In the following sessions, a light warm-up (10 extensions with a 5-kg weight) was performed before the true experimental session. The subjects always received the same instruction "Go until you cannot lift the weight any longer." The weight to be lifted was individually set at 60% of 1-RM. The subjects were instructed to perform the exercise using as constant a pace as possible and full range of motion. The number of completed extensions was counted and recorded (see Figure 1).

The total work (W) performed was calculated according to the following formula:

$$W = n \times m \times k_1 \times k_2,$$

where n is the number of extensions, m the mass of the load, expressed in kg, raised during the lifting phase of the exercise, k_1 is a constant that is represented by the distance the weight was raised, expressed in meters (0.58 m), and k_2 is gravity acceleration (9.81 m s^{-2}). The subjective rate of perceived exertion (RPE) was assessed verbally every three extensions by using a numerical Borg scale ranging from 6 = rest to 20 = maximal exertion (Borg, 1998). In the $P_{50\%}$ and $P_{25\%}$ groups subjective expectations were evaluated before and after the exercise by asking the subjects which beverage they believed to have drunk. In the control and deceived groups expectations were not specifically evaluated.

In Experiment 1 (verbal suggestions only), the subjects of groups NT_1 and $CAFF_{1\text{-}0\%}$ (controls) and $CAFF_{1\text{-}100\%}$, $CAFF_{1\text{-}50\%}$, $CAFF_{1\text{-}25\%}$ (placebo groups) were tested in two sessions, three days apart (see Figure 1A). In session 1, the baseline performance was assessed. In session 2, the subjects of group NT (control) performed the exercise as in the baseline condition, whereas the subjects of group $CAFF_{1\text{-}0\%}$ received the placebo caffeine, with expectation of no improvement. The subjects of the three placebo groups received the placebo caffeine, along with specific suggestion of increased performance (100, 50, or 25% probability of motor improvement, see Section on Experimental Groups) 15 min before the beginning of the experiment. To increase expectations of better performance, several scientific papers on the topic were shown to the subject during the 15-min interval after placebo, which the subjects believed to be necessary for gastric absorption of caffeine.

In Experiment 2 (verbal suggestions plus conditioning), groups NT_2 and $CAFF_{2\text{-}0\%}$ (controls) and $CAFF_{2\text{-}100\%}$, $CAFF_{2\text{-}50\%}$, $CAFF_{2\text{-}25\%}$ (placebo groups) were tested in four different sessions, three days apart (see Figure 1B). In session 1, the baseline performance was assessed, whereas in sessions 2 and 3 a conditioning procedure was

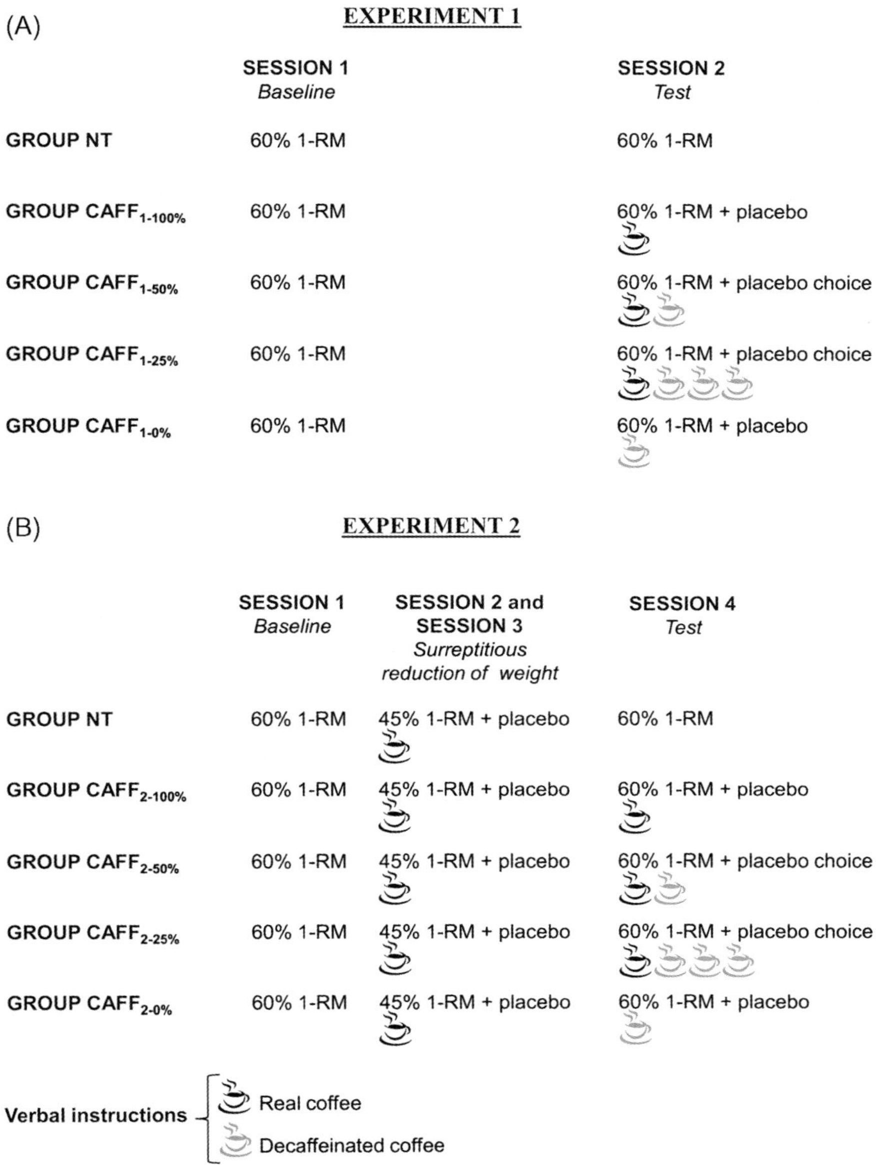

Figure 1. (A) Paradigm of Experiment 1 (verbal suggestions only), (B) Paradigm of Experiment 2 (verbal suggestions plus conditioning).

carried out (Voudouris, Peck, & Coleman, 1989, 1990). This consisted in administering the placebo caffeine along with the suggestion of increased muscle performance, according to the same procedure of Experiment 1. But after this, the weight was surreptitiously lowered to 45% of 1-RM, out of the subject sight, so as to make the subjects believe that the "ergogenic agent" was highly effective. In session 4, all subjects performed the exercise with the weight restored to 60% of 1-RM, as in the baseline condition. In this last session, group NT_2 (control) was given no drink, group 0% received the placebo caffeine without expectation of improvement and the three placebo groups received the placebo caffeine with specific suggestions of better performance (100, 50, or 25% probability of motor improvement), as in Experiment 1.

Statistical Analysis

Statistical analysis of the muscle work data was performed by means of a balanced design two-ways mixed ANOVA for repeated measures followed by the *post hoc* Student-Neumann-Keuls test for multiple comparisons. The factor "group" was the between variable with five levels (NT, $CAFF_{100\%}$, $CAFF_{50\%}$, $CAFF_{25\%}$, and $CAFF_{0\%}$) whereas the within group variable was the experimental session

Table 2. Work performed (kJ)

Protocol 1 (verbal suggestions only)		
Groups	Work performed (kJ)	
	Session 1	Session 2
NT_1	3.63 ± 0.55	3.63 ± 0.64
$CAFF_{1\text{-}100\%}$	4.37 ± 1.67	4.87 ± 1.91
$CAFF_{1\text{-}50\%}$	4.51 ± 0.93	5.13 ± 1.15
$CAFF_{1\text{-}25\%}$	4.94 ± 1.75	5.42 ± 1.92
$CAFF_{1\text{-}0\%}$	5.10 ± 1.88	5.42 ± 1.63

Protocol 2 (verbal suggestions + conditioning)				
Groups	Work performed (kJ)			
	Session 1	Session 2	Session 3	Session 4
NT_2	4.02 ± 1.46	4.56 ± 1.61	5.02 ± 1.91	4.38 ± 1.61
$CAFF_{2\text{-}100\%}$	4.51 ± 0.98	5.42 ± 1.22	5.84 ± 1.44	5.50 ± 1.49
$CAFF_{2\text{-}50\%}$	4.81 ± 1.39	6.02 ± 2.41	6.74 ± 3.04	5.75 ± 1.44
$CAFF_{2\text{-}25\%}$	4.74 ± 1.55	6.05 ± 1.76	6.71 ± 1.86	5.75 ± 1.73
$CAFF_{2\text{-}0\%}$	5.09 ± 1.25	6.41 ± 2.20	6.98 ± 2.64	5.73 ± 1.90

(baseline vs. session 2 or baseline vs. session 4). The ANOVA for repeated measures, followed by the *post hoc* Student-Neumann-Keuls test for multiple comparisons, was used for RPE analysis. Data are presented as mean ± standard deviation (*SD*), and the level of significance was set at $p < .05$.

Results

Experiment 1 (Verbal Suggestions Only)

In the first experiment, the ANOVA showed that the subjects in the five groups did not differ for age ($p = .66$), weight ($p = .89$), height ($p = .45$), body mass index (BMI; $p = .48$) or RM-1 ($p = .08$), or weight lifted ($p = .07$) (Table 1).

The work performed by groups NT_1, $CAFF_{1\text{-}100\%}$, $CAFF_{1\text{-}50\%}$, $CAFF_{1\text{-}25\%}$, and $CAFF_{1\text{-}0\%}$ in session 1 (baseline) and 2 (test, when expectation of performance improvement was induced with different probabilities of caffeine intake) is summarized in Table 2 and illustrated in Figure 2.

The two-way mixed ANOVA for repeated measures within subjects showed significant differences between sessions ($F(1) = 25.67$, $p < .001$). Multiple comparisons with the post hoc Student-Newman-Keuls test showed no differences between session 1 and 2 in the NT_1 ($p = .993$) and $CAFF_{1\text{-}0\%}$ ($p = .159$) groups, but significant differences between session 1 and 2 in the $CAFF_{1\text{-}100\%}$ (11.8% improvement, $p = .012$) and $CAFF_{1\text{-}50\%}$ (14.2% improvement, $p = .006$) groups. Only a tendency to improvement was observed in the $CAFF_{1\text{-}25\%}$ (9.6%, $p = .052$).

The raw data of the RPE in the first experiment are reported in Table 3, and its time-course is shown in Figure 3. A significant decrease in perceived fatigue in session 2 was present only in the $CAFF_{1\text{-}50\%}$ group at the first five measurements, as assessed by means of the post hoc Student-Neumann-Keuls test ($p = .026$ at extension 3; $p < .007$ at extension 6, 9, 12; $p = .014$ at extension 15). Assessments after the 15th extension were not compared due to the uneven number of data.

Experiment 2 (Verbal Suggestions Plus Conditioning)

In the second experiment, the ANOVA showed that the subjects in the five groups did not differ for age ($p = .08$), weight ($p = .54$), height ($p = .36$), body mass index (BMI; $p = .36$), RM-1 ($p = .83$), or weight lifted ($p = .83$) (see Table 1).

The work performed by groups NT_2, $CAFF_{2\text{-}100\%}$, $CAFF_{2\text{-}50\%}$, $CAFF_{2\text{-}25\%}$, and $CAFF_{2\text{-}0\%}$ in session 1 (baseline), 2 and 3 (conditioning, when the load was surreptitiously reduced), and 4 (test, when expectation of performance improvement was induced with different probabilities of caffeine intake) is summarized in Table 2 and illustrated in Figure 4.

The two-way mixed ANOVA for repeated measures showed significant differences between sessions ($F(1) = 33.53$, $p < .001$). In fact, multiple comparisons with the post hoc Student-Newman-Keuls test showed no differences between session 1 and 4 in the NT_2 ($p = .233$) and $CAFF_{2\text{-}0\%}$ ($p = .154$) groups, but significant differences between session 1 and 4 in the $CAFF_{2\text{-}100\%}$ (22.1% improvement, $p = .015$), $CAFF_{2\text{-}50\%}$ (21.3% improvement, $p = .034$), and $CAFF_{2\text{-}25\%}$ groups (22.3% improvement, $p = .020$).

The raw data of the RPE in the second experiment are reported in Table 3, and its time-course is shown in Figure 5. In the control groups (NT_2 and $CAFF_{2\text{-}0\%}$) there were no significant differences between session 1 and 4, whereas only in the $CAFF_{2\text{-}100\%}$ group significant

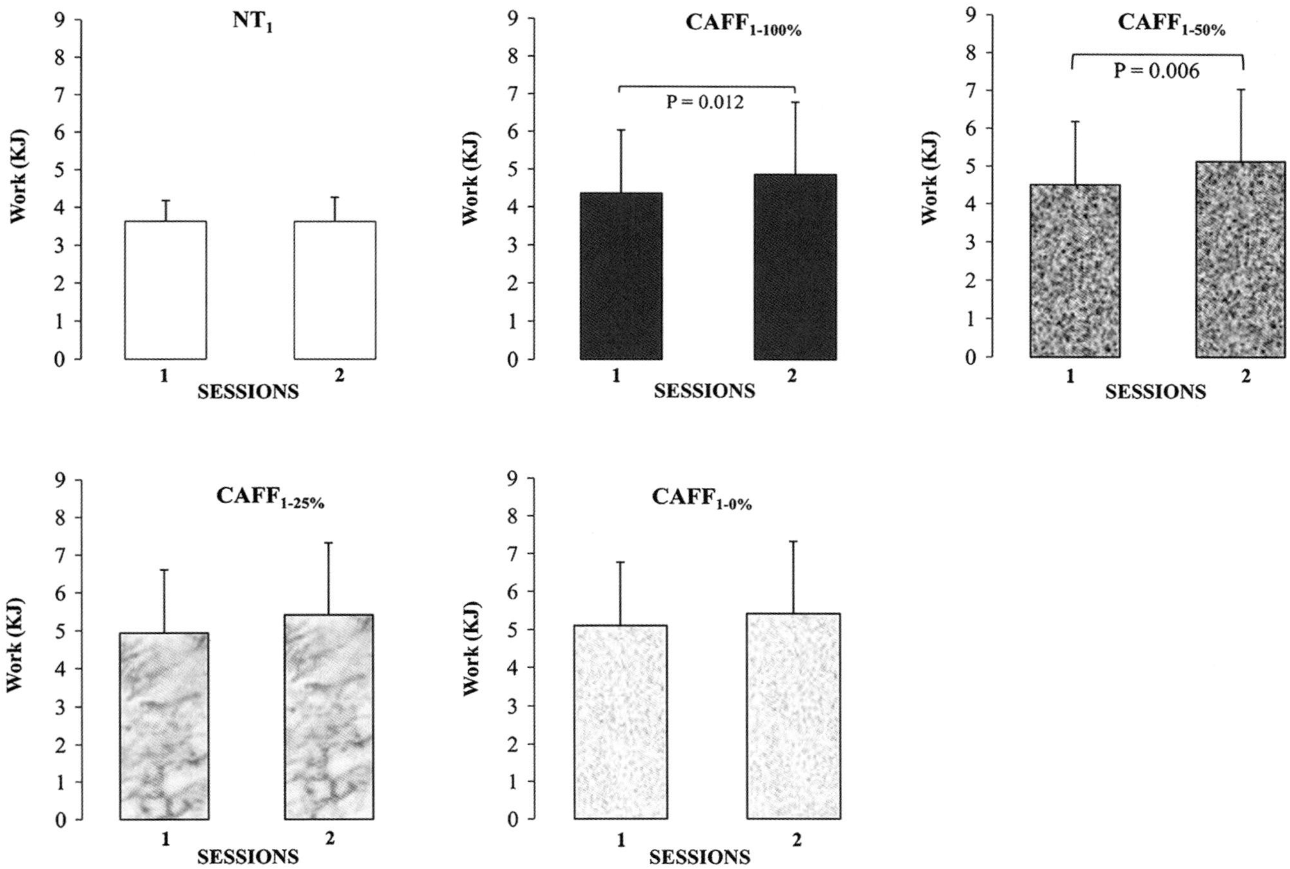

Figure 2. Work (expressed in kJ) performed in Experiment 1 (verbal suggestions only) in the control (NT_1) and placebo groups ($CAFF_{1\text{-}0\%}$, $CAFF_{1\text{-}25\%}$, $CAFF_{1\text{-}50\%}$, $CAFF_{1\text{-}100\%}$).

differences were found between session 1 and 4 at the first five measurements, as assessed by means of the *post hoc* Student-Neumann-Keuls test ($p = .011$ at extension 3; $p < .008$ at extension 6, 9, 12, and 15). Subsequent assessments were not compared, due to the uneven number of data beyond the 15th extension.

Discussion

The main findings of this study can be summarized as follows: (1) by measuring muscle performance during volitional maximal effort, a significant placebo response induced by verbal suggestions alone was observed when the assumed probability of caffeine intake was 50 or 100%, but not when it was as low as 25%. However, when verbal suggestions were reinforced by conditioning, the placebo response was produced in all cases, regardless of the assumed probability of caffeine intake; (2) in no case did we observe any placebo response in the 0% groups, that is, when decaffeinated coffee was administered with the open instruction that it was only a placebo; (3) by measuring the rate of perceived exertion (RPE) the placebo response was observed more sporadically, only in the 50% group with verbal suggestions alone and only in the 100% group with verbal suggestions associated with conditioning.

On the whole, the strength of verbal suggestions of motor improvement seems not to be a determining factor in the production of the placebo motor response. In fact, not only is the response present regardless of the level of outcome certainty (100% and 50% groups in the verbal suggestions alone experiment and 100%, 50%, and 25% groups in the verbal suggestions plus conditioning experiment), but the placebo response size does not depend on it either (being 14.2 and 11.8% in the 50 and 100% groups, respectively, for the verbal suggestions alone experiment, and 22.3, 21.3, and 22.1% in the 25, 50, and 100% groups, respectively, for the verbal suggestions plus conditioning experiment). This differs from the graded placebo analgesia observed in the clinical context, where deceit was associated with a stronger response (Pollo et al. 2001). It could be speculated that the rational calculation of actual probability is not the only factor determining the final level of expectation and in a clinical situation involving pain release emotional factors or anxiety about not receiving the real treatment may play a stronger role.

Table 3. Rates of perceived exertion

Protocol 1 (verbal suggestions only)

	NT_1		$CAFF_{1\text{-}100\%}$		$CAFF_{1\text{-}50\%}$	
Repetition number	S1 (baseline)	S2 (evaluation)	S1 (baseline)	S2 (evaluation)	S1 (baseline)	S2 (evaluation)
3	11.27 ± 3.72	11.32 ± 3.13	9.64 ± 2.58	9.54 ± 2.11	10.36 ± 1.91	9.09 ± 1.45
6	12.82 ± 3.43	12.64 ± 2.84	11.64 ± 2.62	11.23 ± 1.99	12.82 ± 2.09	11.45 ± 1.92
9	14.18 ± 3.34	13.82 ± 2.71	13.27 ± 2.45	12.77 ± 2.32	14.64 ± 2.06	12.82 ± 2.04
12	15.09 ± 3.08	15.55 ± 2.77	15.27 ± 2.72	14.87 ± 2.57	16.18 ± 2.18	14.73 ± 2.45
15	16.91 ± 2.47	17.00 ± 2.41	16.60 ± 2.41	16.55 ± 2.66	17.36 ± 2.06	16.18 ± 2.18
18					18.30 ± 1.09	17.10 ± 1.45
21					19.25 ± 0.42	18.60 ± 1.07

	$CAFF_{1\text{-}25\%}$		$CAFF_{1\text{-}0\%}$	
Repetition number	S1 (baseline)	S2 (evaluation)	S1 (baseline)	S2 (evaluation)
3	9.82 ± 2.40	9.36 ± 2.29	10.36 ± 3.26	9.36 ± 2.62
6	11.73 ± 2.24	11.82 ± 1.83	12.45 ± 3.14	11.27 ± 2.24
9	13.64 ± 2.01	13.45 ± 1.51	14.27 ± 2.97	13.09 ± 2.59
12	15.45 ± 1.75	14.73 ± 1.49	15.86 ± 2.79	14.73 ± 2.20
15	15.82 ± 4.09	16.64 ± 1.43	15.73 ± 5.35	16.27 ± 2.20
18	18.09 ± 1.38	17.73 ± 1.79	18.18 ± 1.60	17.82 ± 1.60
21	18.70 ± 0.82	18.20 ± 1.55	18.80 ± 1.03	18.50 ± 0.71

Protocol 2 (verbal suggestions + conditioning)

	NT_2				$CAFF_{2\text{-}100\%}$				$CAFF_{2\text{-}50\%}$			
Repetition number	S1 (baseline)	S2 (conditioning)	S3 (conditioning)	S4 (evaluation)	S1 (baseline)	S2 (conditioning)	S3 (conditioning)	S4 (evaluation)	S1 (baseline)	S2 (conditioning)	S3 (conditioning)	S4 (evaluation)
3	11.09 ± 2.17	9.82 ± 2.48	10.00 ± 1.95	11.09 ± 2.70	11.18 ± 2.68	9.09 ± 2.39	9.73 ± 2.76	10.05 ± 2.72	10.36 ± 3.23	9.91 ± 2.63	9.82 ± 2.40	10.82 ± 3.12
6	12.91 ± 1.76	11.73 ± 2.57	11.45 ± 2.16	13.00 ± 2.49	12.59 ± 2.56	10.45 ± 2.34	10.91 ± 2.84	11.45 ± 2.58	12.55 ± 3.01	11.55 ± 2.42	11.36 ± 2.50	12.91 ± 3.24
9	14.82 ± 1.66	13.09 ± 2.34	13.09 ± 1.87	14.82 ± 2.27	14.27 ± 2.41	12.00 ± 2.53	12.18 ± 2.64	12.91 ± 2.59	14.09 ± 2.95	12.73 ± 2.41	12.82 ± 2.23	14.09 ± 2.70
12	16.82 ± 1.72	14.45 ± 2.02	14.73 ± 2.20	16.64 ± 2.20	15.73 ± 2.69	13.00 ± 2.57	13.36 ± 2.29	14.27 ± 2.24	15.91 ± 2.17	14.09 ± 2.47	13.73 ± 2.10	15.36 ± 2.20
15	18.27 ± 1.35	16.00 ± 2.05	16.09 ± 2.07	17.73 ± 1.95	17.18 ± 2.18	14.27 ± 2.37	14.36 ± 2.29	15.73 ± 1.85	17.68 ± 1.68	15.55 ± 1.81	15.00 ± 1.73	16.73 ± 1.68
18									18.64 ± 1.12	16.64 ± 1.43	25.18 ± 30.83	18.00 ± 1.00
21									19.27 ± 0.47	17.82 ± 1.08	17.18 ± 1.60	18.70 ± 0.67

	$CAFF_{2\text{-}25\%}$				$CAFF_{2\text{-}0\%}$			
Repetition number	S1 (baseline)	S2 (conditioning)	S3 (conditioning)	S4 (evaluation)	S1 (baseline)	S2 (conditioning)	S3 (conditioning)	S4 (evaluation)
3	10.18 ± 1.94	9.09 ± 2.17	9.45 ± 2.11	9.91 ± 2.21	9.55 ± 2.30	9.27 ± 1.95	8.73 ± 2.00	9.36 ± 2.29
6	12.55 ± 1.75	10.91 ± 2.12	11.27 ± 1.79	11.91 ± 2.47	12.27 ± 2.15	11.27 ± 1.90	10.55 ± 1.86	11.82 ± 1.78
9	14.00 ± 2.32	12.45 ± 1.97	12.36 ± 2.01	13.45 ± 3.08	13.82 ± 2.14	12.73 ± 2.10	12.27 ± 1.62	13.91 ± 1.30
12	15.55 ± 2.66	13.45 ± 2.46	13.64 ± 2.62	14.55 ± 3.05	15.64 ± 2.01	14.09 ± 1.58	13.64 ± 1.63	15.64 ± 1.63
15	17.45 ± 2.11	14.73 ± 2.33	14.45 ± 2.42	15.73 ± 2.80	17.09 ± 1.70	15.27 ± 1.74	15.09 ± 1.81	17.00 ± 1.41
18	18.10 ± 1.79	16.27 ± 2.53	15.64 ± 2.84	16.82 ± 2.64	18.27 ± 1.35	16.64 ± 1.69	16.36 ± 1.57	18.09 ± 1.45
21	18.67 ± 1.66	17.27 ± 2.33	16.73 ± 2.33	17.50 ± 2.12	19.10 ± 0.99	17.36 ± 1.86	17.09 ± 1.51	18.73 ± 1.01

Note. S = session.

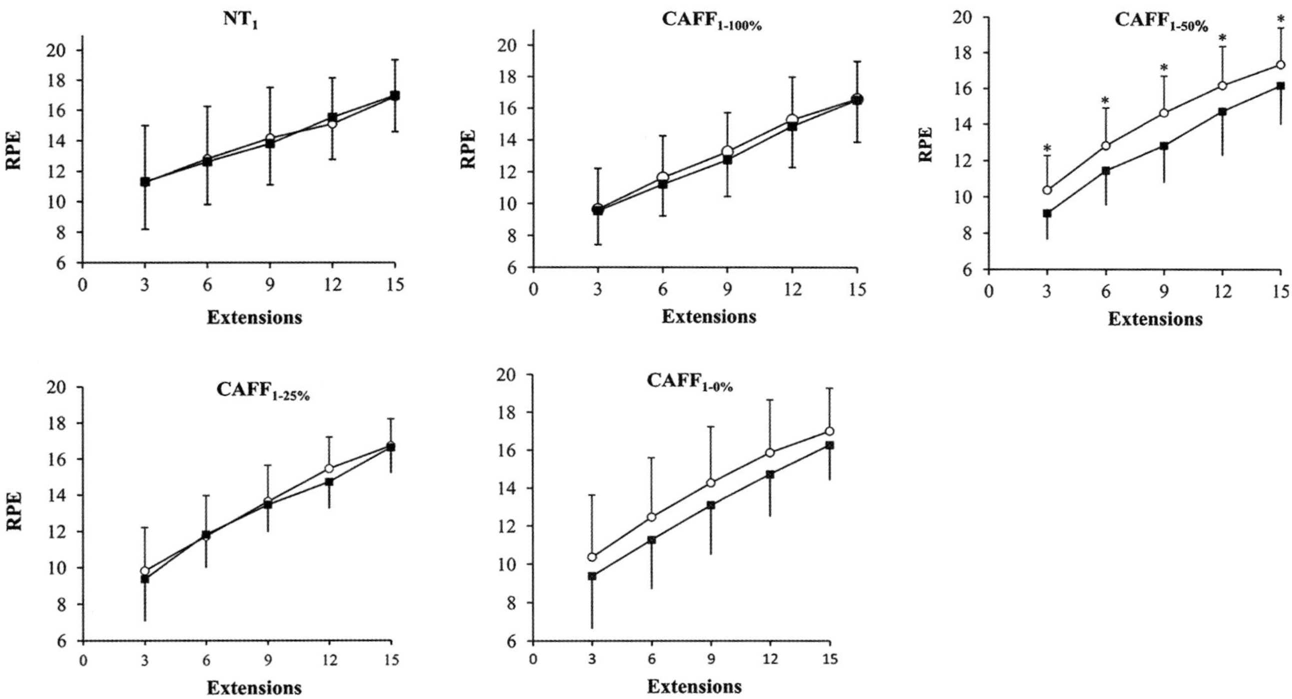

Figure 3. Rate of perceived exertion (RPE) time course, expressed on the Borg scale (from 6 to 20), in Experiment 1 (verbal suggestions only) in the control group (NT_1) and in the placebo groups ($CAFF_{1\text{-}0\%}$, $CAFF_{1\text{-}25\%}$, $CAFF_{1\text{-}50\%}$, $CAFF_{1\text{-}100\%}$).

Assessing the impact of verbal suggestions on the placebo response is of great importance also for clinical trials, because patient expectations can influence trial outcome. For example, it has been reported in pain studies that group assignment (to real or sham treatment) was unrelated to effect on pain, but if subjects were regrouped according to perceived rather than real group assignment, significant less pain for those subjects believing to be in the real treatment group could be shown (Bausell, Lao, Bergman, Lee, & Berman, 2005; Linde et al., 2007). In clinical trials, patients blinded to group allocation typically face a 50% probability of receiving either the placebo or the active drug, but in the design of trials with differing probabilities the ensuing modulation of expectation and its potential influence on the placebo response should be taken into account.

Our results also support the important role of conditioning in shaping the placebo response. Conditioning may act by an independent mechanism or provide a means to reinforce conscious expectations of improvement (Kirsch, Lynn, Vigorito, & Miller, 2004, Rescorla, 1988), but it represents in any case a learning phenomenon enabling conditioned subjects to show more prominent placebo responses than unconditioned ones (Amanzio & Benedetti, 1999; Colloca et al., 2008). In our experiment, adding conditioning to a low verbal suggestions of motor improvement, in itself insufficient to induce the placebo response (25% group in Exp. 1), resulted in the production of an observable motor improvement. This is relevant for the placebo-responsiveness issue, as it adds on the knowledge that previous experience may be a key determinant of a subject's responsiveness, possibly also in the clinical context (Colloca & Benedetti, 2006).

Interestingly, we did not observe any placebo response in the 0% groups, which differ from the NT groups only in the fact that they did receive a cup of decaffeinated coffee, with the clear instruction that it was only a placebo. In a similar "open-label" placebo protocol, Kaptchuk et al. (2010) reported the occurrence of subjective symptom improvement in irritable bowel syndrome (IBS) patients. The discrepancy is in our opinion only apparent: In fact, in the IBS study the patients were instructed that the sugar pills "had been shown in clinical studies to produce significant improvement in IBS symptoms through mind-body self-healing processes," and in so doing they elicited expectations. In our study on the other hand, we explicitly told the subjects that the procedure was useless. Even when our subjects had been conditioned to the efficacy of the caffeine drinking procedure, the conscious knowledge of its uselessness was enough to counteract any placebo response possibly resulting from pure unconscious conditioning. This is in agreement with the observation that nocebo suggestions of hyperalgesia can reverse conditioning-induced placebo analgesia, but it must be noted that when the physiological response is unconscious, as with immune or endocrine responses, modulation by expectation does not occur (Benedetti et al., 2003).

Some limitations of this study must be acknowledged. First, we did not measure the subjects' expectations, thus limiting our interpretation to the influence of different

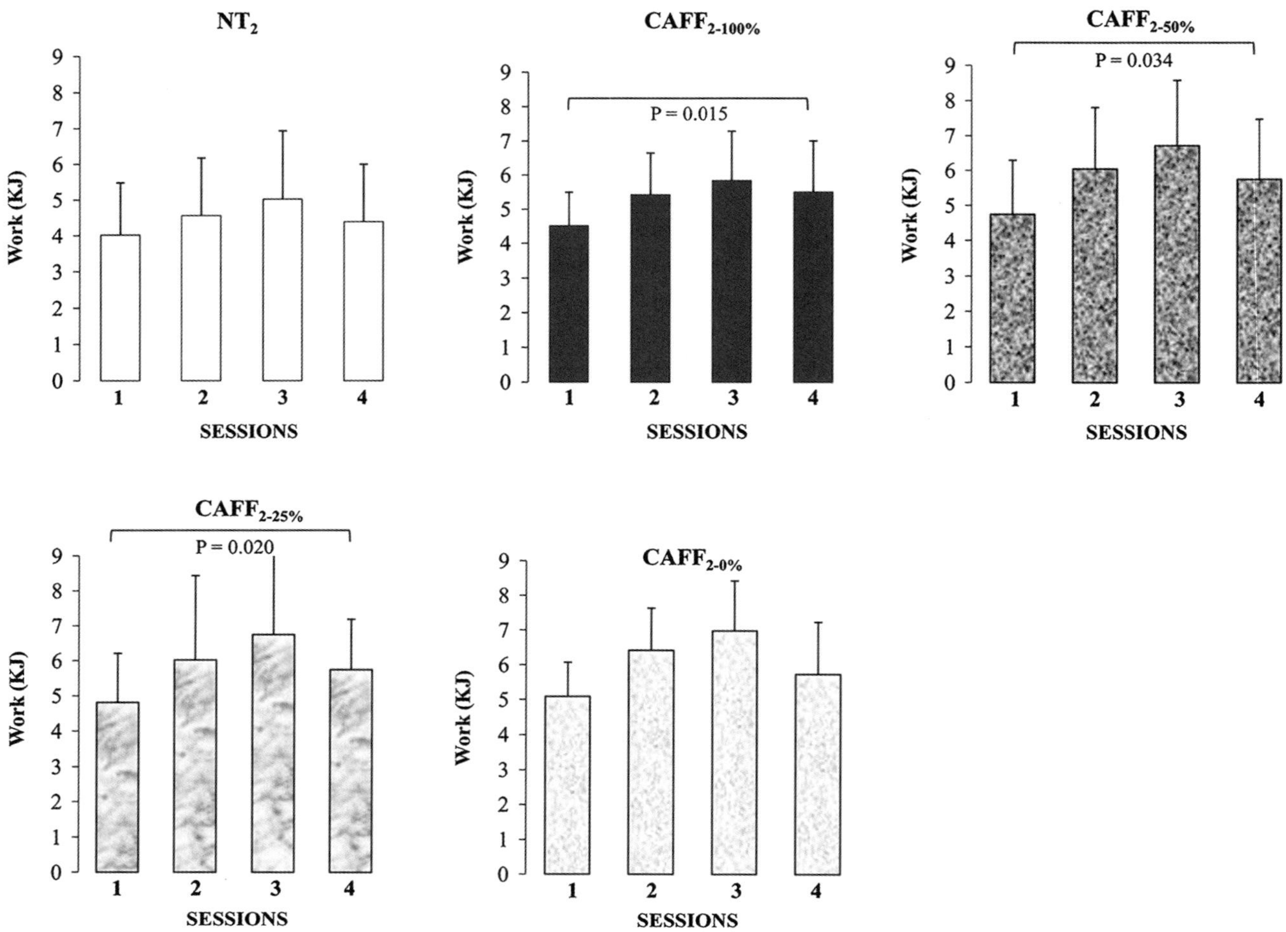

Figure 4. Work (expressed in kJ) performed in Experiment 2 (verbal suggestions plus conditioning) in the control (NT_2) and placebo groups ($CAFF_{2\text{-}0\%}$, $CAFF_{2\text{-}25\%}$, $CAFF_{2\text{-}50\%}$, $CAFF_{2\text{-}100\%}$). In the conditioning sessions 2 and 3, the load was reduced, whereas it was the same in sessions 1 and 4.

verbal information on motor performance rather than the influence of different expectations on motor performance. Even if subjects in the 50% and 25% groups were asked which beverage they believed to have drunk, only half of subjects answered the question, thus not allowing a proper statistical analysis of the data. The second limitation is represented by the low number of participants in each group. For instance, the tendency toward improvement observed in the 25% group might be due to small sample size. However, in this study we used a balanced design, which may be appropriate for detecting significant effects in small samples. Third, besides the objective measurement of work performed, we also recorded the subjective outcome of perceived fatigue in order to compare our results with previous data (Pollo et al., 2012). However, similarly to our study on the nocebo effect in motor performance (Pollo et al., 2010), RPE proved to be less reliable compared with the objective measurement of work performed. This is probably due to the difficulty in rating fatigue, especially during a fast fatigue-developing anaerobic exercise.

The analysis of neurotransmitter release in specific brain areas represents a different approach in the study of the role of outcome certainty in the placebo response. So far, this has been carried out only for dopamine in the ventral striatum of Parkinson patients (Lidstone et al., 2010). Although in this case also the placebo response involved the motor system, it is difficult to draw a comparison with our study, because the neurochemical changes appeared to be related to the expectation (i.e., to the probability of reward, to which the placebo response is likened) rather than to clinical benefit (i.e., the placebo response). Significant motor improvement was observed only at 75% declared probability of receiving active medication, without correlation between dopamine release and motor scores. A recent fMRI study on placebo responsiveness also addressed graded expectations, analyzing behavioral, and neural placebo analgesic responses in a rectal pain model in healthy subjects. Although the data regarding belief strength were not discussed in detail, the response in placebo-responders appears to be a graded phenomenon (Elsenbruch et al., 2012).

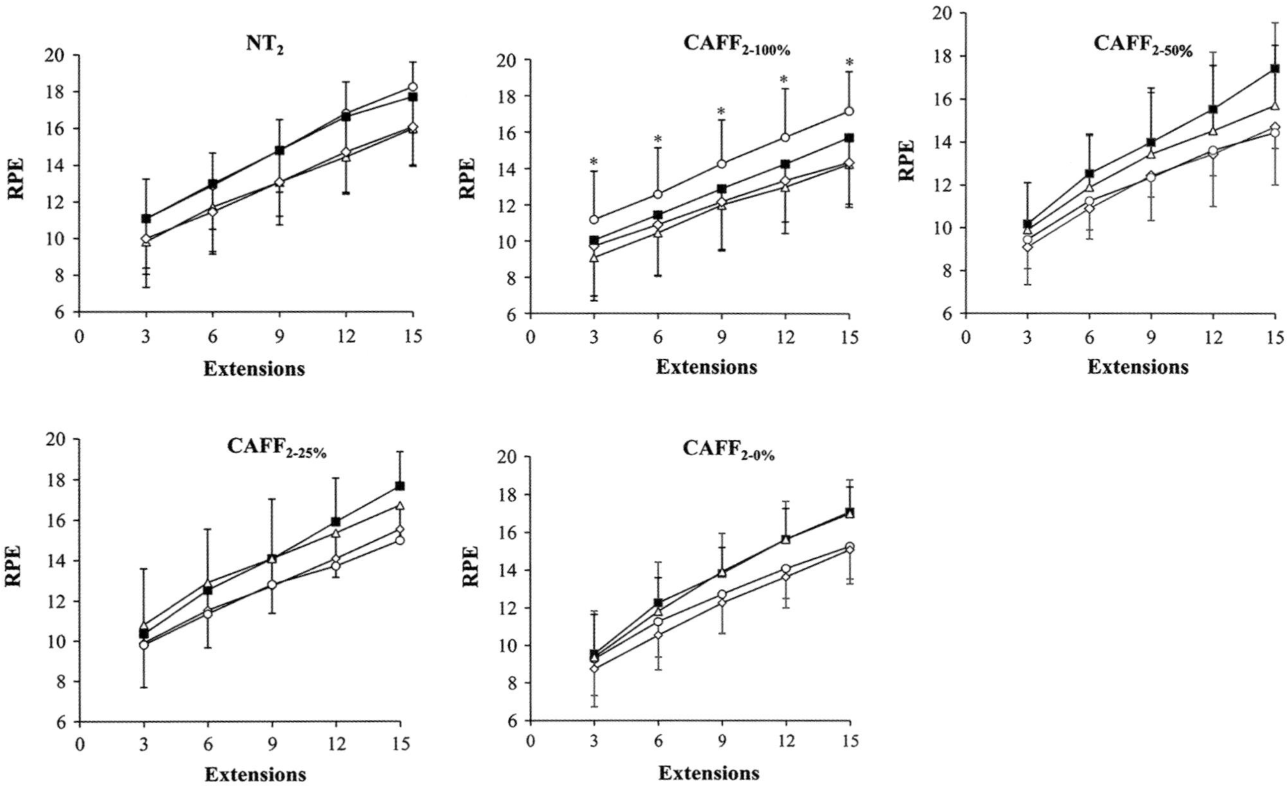

Figure 5. Rate of perceived exertion (RPE) time course in Experiment 2 (verbal suggestion + conditioning), in the control group (NT_2) and in the placebo groups ($CAFF_{2\text{-}0\%}$, $CAFF_{2\text{-}25\%}$, $CAFF_{2\text{-}50\%}$, $CAFF_{2\text{-}100\%}$). In the conditioning sessions 2 and 3, the load was reduced, whereas it was the same in sessions 1 and 4.

Placebo effects on maximal volitional effort should be viewed in the context of central fatigue regulation. Recently, fatigue has been proposed to be a "brain-derived emotion that regulates the exercise behavior to ensure the protection of whole body homeostasis" (Noakes, 2012). According to this formulation, a central governor of fatigue made-up of a distributed network with feed-forward and feed-back components integrates sensory, metabolic, emotional, motivational, and cognitive factors and continuously supervises motor output production. Proper recruitment of motor units allows muscle contraction, which is however always kept at submaximal levels in order to maintain a reserve and to prevent homeostasis failure. Activation of a number of brain regions has been reported in association with the raising sense of effort during exercise and/or the decision to terminate it, among which the insular cortex, the anterior cingulate cortex (ACC), the medial prefrontal cortex, and thalamic regions (Hilty, Jäncke, Luechinger, Boutellier, & Lutz, 2011; Williamson, Fadel, & Mitchell, 2006). Interestingly, these are all regions also implicated in placebo analgesia (Eippert et al., 2009; Wager et al., 2004). Even in the absence of more direct evidence, such as could be provided by imaging studies, it is tempting to speculate that placebo procedures may affect the central governor activity, and our data would support the fact that they act by mechanisms similar to those involved in placebo analgesia, for example, anticipation of future outcome (in this case a modulation of fatigue) or previous experience (conditioning).

Acknowledgments

This work was supported by grants by the Volkswagen Foundation and by Regione Piemonte.

References

Amanzio, M., & Benedetti, F. (1999). Neuropharmacological dissection of placebo analgesia: Expectation-activated opioid systems versus conditioning-activated specific subsystems. *Journal of Neuroscience, 19*, 484–494.

Bausell, R. B., Lao, L., Bergman, S., Lee, W. L., & Berman, B. M. (2005). Is acupuncture analgesia an expectancy effect? *Evaluation and the Health Professions, 28*, 9–26.

Beedie, C. J., Coleman, D. A., & Foad, A. J. (2007). Positive and negative placebo effects resulting from the deceptive administration of an ergogenic aid. *International Journal of Sport Nutrition and Exercise Metabolism, 17*, 259–269.

Beedie, C. J., & Foad, A. J. (2009). The placebo effect in sport performance: A brief review. *Sports Medicine, 39*, 313–329.

Benedetti, F. (2008). *Placebo effects: Understanding the mechanisms in health and disease*. Oxford, UK: Oxford University Press.

Benedetti, F., Amanzio, M., Rosato, R., & Blanchard, C. (2011). Nonopioid placebo analgesia in mediated by CB1 cannabinoid receptors. *Nature Medicine, 17*, 1228–1230.

Benedetti, F., Pollo, A., & Colloca, L. (2007). Opioid-mediated placebo responses boost pain endurance and physical performance: Is it doping in sport competitions? *Journal of Neuroscience, 27*, 11934–11939.

Benedetti, F., Pollo, A., Lopiano, L., Lanotte, M., Vighetti, S., & Rainero, I. (2003). Conscious expectation and unconscious conditioning in analgesic, motor and hormonal placebo/nocebo responses. *Journal of Neuroscience, 23*, 4315–4323.

Bingel, U., Wanigasekera, V., Wiech, K., Mhuircheartaigh, R. N., Lee, M. C., Ploner, M., & Tracey, I. (2011). The effect of treatment expectation on drug efficacy: Imaging the analgesic benefit of the opioid remifentanil. *Science Translational Medicine, 3*, 70ra14. doi: 10.1126/scitranslmed.3001244

Borg, G. (1998). *Borg's perceived exertion and pain scales*. Champaign, IL: Human Kinetics.

Colloca, L., & Benedetti, F. (2006). How prior experience shapes placebo analgesia. *Pain, 124*, 126–133.

Colloca, L., Tinazzi, M., Recchia, S., Le Pera, D., Fiaschi, A., Benedetti, F., & Valeriani, M. (2008). Learning potentiates neurohysiological and behavioral placebo analgesic responses. *Pain, 139*, 306–314.

de la Fuente-Fernandez, R., Ruth, T. J., Sossi, V., Schulzer, M., Calne, D. B., & Stoessl, A. J. (2001). Expectation and dopamine release: Mechanism of the placebo effect in Parkinson's disease. *Science, 293*, 1164–1166.

Eippert, F., Bingel, U., Schoell, E. D., Yacubian, J., Klinger, R., Lorenz, J., & Büchel, C. (2009). Activation of the opioidergic descending pain control system underlies placebo analgesia. *Neuron, 63*, 533–543.

Elsenbruch, S., Kotsis, V., Benson, S., Rosenberger, C., Reidick, D., Schedlowski, M., ... Gizewki, E. R. (2012). Neural mechanisms mediating the effects of expectation in visceral placebo analgesia: An fMRI study in healthy placebo responders and nonresponders. *Pain, 153*, 382–390.

Hilty, L., Jäncke, L., Luechinger, R., Boutellier, U., & Lutz, K. (2011). Limitation of physical performance in a muscle fatiguing handgrip exercise is mediated by thalamo-insular activity. *Human Brain Mapping, 32*, 2151–2160.

Kalmar, J. M., & Cafarelli, E. (1999). Effects of caffeine on neuromuscular function. *Journal of Applied Physiology, 87*, 801–808.

Kaptchuk, T. J., Friedlander, E., Kelley, J. M., Sanchez, M. N., Kokkotou, E., Singer, J. P., ... Lembo, A. J. (2010). Placebos without deception: A randomized controlled trial in irritable bowel syndrome. *PLoS One, 5*, e15591. doi: 10.1371/journal.pone.0015591

Kirsch, I., Lynn, S. J., Vigorito, M., & Miller, R. R. (2004). The role of cognition in classical and operant conditioning. *Journal of Clinical Psychology, 60*, 369–392.

Kirsch, I., & Weixel, L. J. (1988). Double-blind versus deceptive administration of a placebo. *Behavioral Neuroscience, 1023*, 19–323.

Lidstone, S. C., Schulzer, M., Dinelle, K., Mak, E., Sossi, V., Ruth, T. J., ... Stoessl, A. J. (2010). Effects of expectation on placebo-induced dopamine release in Parkinson disease. *Archives of General Psychiatry, 67*, 857–865.

Linde, K., Witt, C. M., Streng, A., Weidenhammer, W., Wagenpheil, S., Brinkhaus, B., ... Melchart, D. (2007). The impact of patient expectations on outcomes in four randomized controlled trials of acupuncture in patients with chronic pain. *Pain, 128*, 264–271.

Lui, F., Colloca, L., Duzzi, D., Anchisi, D., Benedetti, F., & Porro, C. A. (2010). Neural bases of conditioned placebo analgesia. *Pain, 151*, 816–824.

Noakes, D. T. (2012). Fatigue is a brain-derived emotion that regulates the exercise behavior to ensure the protection of whole body homeostasis. *Frontiers in Physiology, 3*, 82.

Petrovic, P., Kalso, E., Petersson, K. M., & Ingvar, M. (2002). Placebo and opioid analgesia – Imaging a shared neuronal network. *Science, 295*, 1737–1740.

Pollo, A., Amanzio, M., Arslanian, A., Casadio, C., Maggi, G., & Benedetti, F. (2001). Response expectancies in placebo analgesia and their clinical relevance. *Pain, 93*, 77–84.

Pollo, A., Carlino, E., & Benedetti, F. (2008). The top-down influence of ergogenic placebos on muscle work and fatigue. *European Journal of Neuroscience, 28*, 379–388.

Pollo, A., Carlino, E., & Benedetti, F. (2011). Placebo mechanisms across different conditions: From the clinical setting to physical performance. *Philosophical Transaction of the Royal Society of London B Biological Sciences, 366*, 1790–1798.

Pollo, A., Carlino, E., Vase, L., & Benedetti, F. (2012). Preventing motor training through nocebo suggestions. *European Journal of Applied Physiology, 112*, 3893–3903. doi: 10.1007/s00421-012-2333-9

Price, D. D., Finniss, D. G., & Benedetti, F. (2008). A comprehensive review of the placebo effect: Recent advances and current thought. *Annual Reviews of Psychology, 59*, 565–590.

Rescorla, R. A. (1988). Pavlovian conditioning: It is not what you think it is. *The American Psychologist, 43*, 151–160.

Voudouris, N. J., Peck, C. L., & Coleman, G. (1989). Conditioned response models of placebo phenomena: Further support. *Pain, 38*, 109–116.

Voudouris, N. J., Peck, C. L., & Coleman, G. (1990). The role of conditioning and verbal expectancy in the placebo response. *Pain, 43*, 121–128.

Wager, T. D., Rilling, J. K., Smith, E. E., Sokilik, A., Casey, K. L., Davidson, R. J., ... Cohen, J. D. (2004). Placebo-induced changes in fMRI in the anticipation and experience of pain. *Science, 303*, 1162–1167.

Williamson, J. W., Fadel, P. J., & Mitchell, J. H. (2006). New insights into central cardiovascular control during exercise in humans: A central command update. *Experimental Physiology, 91*, 51–58.

Zubieta, J. K., Bueller, J. A., Jackson, L. R., Scott, D. J., Xu, Y., Koeppe, R. A., ... Stohler, C. S. (2005). Placebo effects mediated by endogenous opioid activity on μ-opioid receptors. *Journal of Neuroscience, 25*, 7754–7762.

Elisa Carlino

Department of Neurosciences
University of Turin
Corso Raffaello 30
10125 Turin
Italy
Tel. +39 011 670-8491
Fax +39 011 670-8174
E-mail elisa.carlino@unito.it

Original Article

Patient Involvement in Treatment Decision Making Can Help or Hinder Placebo Analgesia

The Moderating Role of Prior Experience

Andrew L. Geers, Jason P. Rose, Stephanie L. Fowler, and Jill A. Brown

University of Toledo, Toledo, OH, USA

Abstract. Experiments have found that choosing between placebo analgesics can reduce pain more than being assigned a placebo analgesic. Because earlier research has shown prior experience moderates choice effects in other contexts, we tested whether prior experience with a pain stimulus moderates this placebo-choice association. Before a cold water pain task, participants were either told that an inert cream would reduce their pain or they were not told this information. Additionally, participants chose between one of two inert creams for the task or they were not given choice. Importantly, we also measured prior experience with cold water immersion. Individuals with prior cold water immersion experience tended to display greater placebo analgesia when given choice, whereas participants without this experience tended to display greater placebo analgesia without choice. Prior stimulus experience appears to moderate the effect of choice on placebo analgesia.

Keywords: placebo effect, choice, prior experience, pain, analgesia

Research indicates that placebo effects can be particularly valuable in pain reduction (placebo analgesia; Colloca & Benedetti, 2005; Tracey, 2010). As placebo analgesia varies substantially in magnitude across studies (Vase, Riley, & Price, 2002), researchers have begun searching for factors that moderate this effect (Colloca & Benedetti, 2006). The present study focuses on a contextual variable recently found to moderate placebo analgesia: Treatment choice. By treatment choice we are referring to whether or not an individual has decisional control over a medical treatment rather than having a medical treatment assigned to him/her. Clarifying the role of treatment choice in placebo analgesia is important because patients are often involved in treatment decision making, as evidenced by the availability of web-based medical tools, the development of patient-friendly medical decision aids, and the shift toward shared decision making in health care.

Recent experiments have tested the possibility that treatment choice alters placebo analgesia (Brown, Fowler, Rasinski, Rose, & Geers, 2013; Rose, Geers, Rasinski, & Fowler, 2012). In these experiments participants have reported lower levels of pain when they selected a placebo analgesic as compared to when they were assigned a placebo analgesic by an experimenter. These findings are consistent with the theorizing of Geers and Rose (2011) who proposed that choice over treatment options may strengthen placebo effects because establishing control through choice can reduce anxiety and increase feelings of comfort.

Although the aforementioned studies provide evidence that choice between treatments can increase placebo analgesia, there may be cases when choice does not have this effect. Even though patients frequently want decisional control, it is not always preferred and in some cases decisional control via choice results in greater discomfort and more negative affect (Botti & Iyengar, 2004; Calne, Calne, & Calne, 2009). In particular, when treatment decisions are about serious illnesses or when patients feel unprepared or ill-informed about their ailment or treatment options, choice among treatments can elevate discomfort and reduce treatment satisfaction (Hack, Degner, Watson, & Sinha, 2006). In the context of the present research, it seems possible that treatment choice may not enhance placebo analgesia when choice events increase rather than decrease discomfort (Geers & Rose, 2011).

One factor that may alter comfort levels when selecting between analgesic treatments is if an individual has prior experience with the upcoming form of painful stimulation. We theorized that selecting between treatments without prior experience could make individuals feel unprepared and raise discomfort levels. Having prior experience with a painful stimulus, however, may make individuals feel more informed and comfortable about choosing between placebo analgesics. As such, the present research tested whether prior stimulus experience moderates the influence of treatment choice on placebo analgesia in a laboratory paradigm. Our main hypothesis was that choice would

DOI: 10.1027/2151-2604/a000179

enhance placebo analgesia more when individuals had prior experience with the pain stimulus. Further, we also hypothesized that participants without prior experience would report having high levels of discomfort prior to the pain task when asked to select between (placebo) treatments.

Method

Participants and Design

The study was conducted at a university in the Midwestern region of the United States. The sample consisted of 106 (71 female, 35 male) healthy young adults (M age = 19.56) who participated individually in return for partial course credit. Sixty-three percent reported their race as White/Caucasian, 22.6% as African American, 3.8% as Asian, .9% as Native American, 8.5% as mixed/other, and one participant did not specify race. Four other participants were excluded from the study. Two participants were nonnative English speakers who did not understand the experimental instructions and two participants were excluded because they were already experiencing acute pain due to recent injuries.

Participants were randomly assigned to a condition in a 2(Verbal Expectation) × 2(Choice) between-subjects factorial design. Specifically, prior to a cold pressor pain task, half of the participants were told that a cream applied to their hand would reduce the cold pressor pain, whereas the other half were not given this verbal information. Cross-cutting this manipulation, half of the participants had the opportunity to choose between one of two creams to be used, whereas the other half were assigned a cream. Critically, we also assessed whether or not participants had prior exposure to cold water pain stimulation and used this as a predictor variable in data analysis. All procedures were approved in advance by the University's Institutional Review Board. Participants read and signed an informed consent document at the outset of the study session.

Prior Experience

Prior experience with cold water immersion was assessed by asking participants if they had ever submerged their arm, leg, or hand in ice water for a long period of time. Response options were coded as either "Yes" or "No." Fifty-nine participants responded "Yes" to this question and 47 responded "No." We used this breakdown for our prior experience predictor variable in the subsequent analyses. It should be noted that if participants responded yes to the question, they were further asked to indicate how often they had submerged their arm, leg, or hand in ice water (Geers & Lassiter, 2005). Preliminary examination of these additional data yielded substantial variability and responses did not play a clear role in data analysis.

Procedures

The laboratory sessions were conducted by an experimenter wearing a white lab coat in a room containing an intercom system for room-to-room communication. At the beginning of the study session, participants completed a health history questionnaire and were told that they would be placing their nondominant hand into a container of water and crushed ice (i.e., the cold pressor task).

Participants in the *verbal expectation conditions* were told that the purpose of the experiment was to assess new pain-relieving creams. Two lotion bottles were then presented that were said to contain two different creams (in actuality, both bottles held the same inert lotion). Participants were given a laminated note card that provided brief sham descriptions of the two creams. Specifically, one cream was said to warm an individual's hand, protecting it like a glove, whereas the second cream was said to block pain receptors in the hand. Participants in the *no expectation conditions* were also informed that the study involved pain perception and were presented with the same two bottles. However, these participants were told the bottles contained different sanitizing creams that would remove dirt and oil from their hand before the cold water task. Similar to the verbal expectation participants, the no expectation participants were also presented with a laminated card that provided descriptions of the two creams. One cream was said to be a cleansing agent that contained pure organic in gredients, whereas the second was said to be a product of a United States manufacturer. Importantly, the verbal expectation and no expectation participants went through the same procedure and were both presented with identical lotion bottles. Finally, it should be noted that the presentation order of the two bottle descriptions was counterbalanced.

After explaining the two creams, the experimenter left the room for 2 min, seemingly to gather more study materials. When the experimenter returned, participants in the *choice conditions* were given the opportunity to select which of the two creams they wanted to try during the cold water task. Participants in *no choice conditions* had one of the two creams selected for them by the experimenter (determined by random assignment).

Pain Task and Pain Assessment

Next, the experimenter opened up a bottle and applied a tan medicinal-smelling cream to the participant's nondominant hand from the wrist down. The cream was a blend of iodine, food coloring, oil of thyme, and unscented lotion (see Rose et al., 2012). The experimenter then left the room and gave instructions over an intercom. Approximately 1 min after the application of the cream, participants submerged their nondominant hand (up to their wrist) in a container filled with circulating water and crushed ice set at 8° C. Participants were instructed to keep their hand submerged as long as possible, but were told that they could withdraw their hand if the pain became unbearable. Every 15 s during the task (15, 30, 45, 60, and 75 s), participants vocally rated their current level of pain. These concurrent pain ratings were made on a 0 (*no pain*) to 10 (*worst possible pain*) scale. At 75 s, participants were instructed to remove their hand from the water.

Next, participants reported their pain using the short form of the McGill Pain Questionnaire (SF-MPQ; Melzack, 1987). Specifically, participants indicated the degree to which they experienced 15 sensory and affective pain descriptors (e.g., stabbing, sharp) on a scale ranging from 1 (*none*) to 4 (*severe*). When analyzed separately, the sensory and affective items displayed similar patterns and thus all 15 items were averaged to yield the SF-MPQ total pain score ($\alpha = .91$).

Discomfort Scale and Verbal Expectation Manipulation Checks

A questionnaire given at the end of the study included an item that inquired about the discomfort experienced prior to the pain task. This item read "Prior to the cold water task, how uncomfortable were you about putting your hand in the ice water" (1 = *not at all uncomfortable*; 7 = *very uncomfortable*). This final questionnaire also included two manipulation check questions. To evaluate the verbal expectation manipulation, participants were asked, "How convinced were you that the hand cream would help you cope with the cold water task?" (1 = *not at all*; 7 = *very much*). To evaluate the choice manipulation, participants were asked, "To what extent did you have a choice over which of the two ointments you would use during the cold water task?" (1 = *no choice at all*; 7 = *complete choice*). These questions were asked at the end of the study session so as not to draw participants' attention to the manipulations. After answering these final questions, participants were thanked and debriefed.

Data Analysis Strategy

Responses to the manipulation check and discomfort items were analyzed by submitting them separately to a 2(Verbal Expectation) × 2(Choice) × 2(Prior Experience) between-subjects analysis of variance (ANOVA). Simple effect tests were conducted to decompose any significant interaction effects. To analyze pain from the cold pressor task, we created three different pain variables. For the first pain variable, here called amount of concurrent pain, we averaged the five pain reports participants supplied during the cold pressor task. For the second pain variable, here called change in concurrent pain, we computed the increase – or change – in pain during the pain task by subtracting participants' first concurrent pain rating from their final concurrent pain rating. The third pain variable, here called post-pain scores, were averaged scores on the SF-MPQ total pain scale that was completed after the cold pressor task. These three pain variables were analyzed separately with the same 2 × 2 × 2 ANOVA and simple effect tests used to examine the manipulation check and discomfort data.

Results

Manipulation Checks

Analysis of the expectation manipulation check data yielded only a significant effect of the verbal expectation manipulation, with participants given the verbal expectation ($M = 3.82$; $SD = 2.04$) reporting being more convinced of the effectiveness of the hand cream than no expectation participants ($M = 2.09$; $SD = 1.57$), $F(1, 96) = 23.68$, $p < .001$, $\eta_p^2 = .20$. Analysis of the choice manipulation check data yielded only a significant effect of the choice manipulation, such that choice participants ($M = 6.13$; $SD = 1.64$) reported having greater choice over the hand cream than no choice participants ($M = 1.49$; $SD = 1.46$), $F(1, 95) = 226.30$, $p < .001$, $\eta_p^2 = .70$. These data provide support for the success of the verbal expectation and choice manipulations.

Pain Reports

Amount of Concurrent Pain

Due to an intercom malfunction, the concurrent pain ratings for two participants were lost. When the remaining concurrent pain data were submitted to the 2 × 2 × 2 ANOVA, the analysis yielded only a significant Verbal Expectation × Prior Experience interaction, $F(1, 96) = 4.48$, $p = .03$, $\eta_p^2 = .05$ (see Table 1). Simple effect tests conducted to clarify this interaction revealed that participants without prior experience reported less pain when given the verbal expectation ($M = 3.97$; $SD = 1.99$) than when given no expectation, ($M = 5.33$; $SD = 2.07$), $t(96) = 2.44$, $p = .01$, $d = .67$. For the prior experience participants, the difference between the verbal expectation ($M = 4.44$; $SD = 2.33$) and no expectation conditions ($M = 4.06$; $SD = 1.75$) was not significant, $t(96) = -.67$, $p = .51$, $d = .18$. These analyses indicate that participants without prior experience displayed a placebo effect on the average concurrent pain measure, whereas participants with prior experience did not. Contrary to predictions, choice did not alter this effect.

Change in Concurrent Pain

Next, the ANOVA on changes in concurrent pain revealed a significant effect of the verbal expectation manipulation, $F(1, 95) = 17.99$, $p < .001$, $\eta_p^2 = .16$, as well as the hypothesized three-way interaction, $F(1, 95) = 5.35$, $p = .02$, $\eta_p^2 = .05$ (see Table 1). To decompose this three-way interaction, we conducted simple effect tests. The first test assessed whether individuals with prior experience to the pain stimulus benefited from choice over their placebo

Table 1. Means and standard deviations for outcome variables by prior experience, choice, and expectation

	Concurrent pain mean (*SD*)	Change in concurrent pain mean (*SD*)	Post-pain mean (*SD*)	Discomfort mean (*SD*)
No prior experience				
No choice				
No expectation	5.85 (1.66)	4.93 (2.71)	2.48 (0.73)	3.94 (1.84)
Placebo expectation	3.44 (2.17)	1.57 (2.21)	1.56 (0.37)	2.92 (1.85)
Choice				
No expectation	4.78 (2.37)	4.00 (2.17)	1.82 (0.45)	3.13 (1.81)
Placebo expectation	4.55 (1.69)	3.38 (2.40)	1.94 (0.53)	5.14 (1.61)
Prior experience				
No choice				
No expectation	3.98 (1.56)	4.36 (1.29)	1.72 (0.47)	2.91 (1.64)
Placebo expectation	4.29 (2.46)	3.25 (2.30)	2.01 (0.62)	2.00 (1.04)
Choice				
No expectation	4.13 (1.98)	5.33 (2.19)	2.04 (0.75)	2.77 (1.30)
Placebo expectation	4.62 (2.29)	2.81 (2.36)	1.55 (0.42)	1.82 (1.33)

Note. Higher scores indicate greater pain and discomfort, respectively.

treatment. In line with earlier studies on choice and placebo analgesia, participants with prior experience reported smaller concurrent pain increases in the verbal expectation condition than in the no expectation condition when given choice, $t(95) = 2.67$, $p = .009$, $d = .55$. Without choice, participants with prior exposure did not show this difference between the verbal expectation and no expectation conditions, $t(95) = 1.18$, $p = .24$, $d = .23$. Next, we examined the change in pain reports for individuals without prior experience. The results of these two tests were the reverse of what was found with the prior experience participants. Specifically, when given choice, individuals without prior experience did not differ across expectation conditions, $t(95) = .72$, $p = .47$, $d = .15$. However, individuals without prior experience reported a smaller increase in pain in the verbal expectation condition as compared to the no expectation condition when not given choice, $t(95) = 4.01$, $p < .001$, $d = 1.01$. These results provide evidence that prior experience with a pain stimulus moderates the effect of choice on placebo analgesia.

Post-Pain Scores

The ANOVA on the SF-MPQ scores produced a main effect of verbal expectation, $F(1, 98) = 5.19$, $p = .03$, $\eta_p^2 = .05$, as well as a significant three-way interaction, $F(1, 98) = 16.57$, $p < .001$, $\eta_p^2 = .15$ (see Table 1). Simple effect tests indicated that when given choice, participants with prior experience reported less pain on the SF-MPQ when given a verbal expectation as compared to when given no expectation, $t(98) = 2.09$, $p = .04$, $d = .42$. A second simple effect test indicated that the SF-MPQ scores of the prior experience participants did not differ in the verbal expectation and no expectation condition without choice, $t(98) = 1.22$, $p = .23$, $d = .25$. Next, we examined the SF-MPQ pain scores for individuals without prior experience. The results of these two tests were again quite different from those with the prior experience participants. First, when given choice, individuals without prior exposure did not differ on the SF-MPQ across the expectation conditions, $t(98) = .52$, $p = .61$, $d = .11$. However, without choice, individuals with no prior experience reported less pain on the SF-MPQ when given the verbal expectation as compared to when given no expectation, $t(98) = 4.46$, $p < .001$, $d = .90$.

Discomfort Scores

Analysis of the discomfort data revealed that individuals without prior pain stimulus experience ($M = 3.79$; $SD = 1.93$) reported feeling more uncomfortable before the pain task than individuals with prior experience ($M = 2.38$; $SD = 1.38$), $F(1, 97) = 20.07$, $p < .001$, $\eta_p^2 = .17$ (see Table 1). The ANOVA also produced significant Verbal Expectation × Prior Experience, $F(1, 97) = 5.14$, $p = .03$, $\eta_p^2 = .05$, Verbal Expectation × Choice, $F(1, 97) = 5.61$, $p = .02$, $\eta_p^2 = .06$, and Verbal Expectation × Choice × Prior Experience interactions, $F(1, 98) = 5.93$, $p = .03$, $\eta_p^2 = .06$. Simple effect tests showed that the key difference among conditions was that when individuals without prior experience were given choice over their placebo treatments, they experienced significantly more discomfort than participants in all other groups (all *p*s < .04).

Discussion

Recent experiments found that the opportunity to choose between placebo analgesics can reduce pain more than having no opportunity to choose between placebo analgesics. The present study explored whether prior pain stimulus experience moderated this choice effect. It was theorized that prior experience may reduce discomfort when choosing between treatments and thus could strengthen placebo analgesia. To investigate this possibility, participants who did or did not recall prior experience with a cold water immersion pain stimulus were randomly assigned to a full-factorial design that crossed a verbal pain relief expectation with a choice manipulation.

Overall, the results support the proposed moderating role of prior experience. First, an analysis of the change in participant pain reports during the cold pressor task revealed that choice did enhance placebo analgesia for the prior experience participants. In contrast, however, participants without prior experience displayed greater placebo analgesia on this variable when they were assigned the placebo by an experimenter. This same pattern of results was uncovered on post-task pain reports as well. Moreover, analysis of the discomfort scores revealed that individuals without prior experience with the pain stimulus felt more discomfort than all other groups when they were selecting between placebo analgesics. Taken together, these results suggest that when treatment choice is uncomfortable it will not increase placebo analgesia. Thus, in some situations, such as when individuals have no prior experience with an upcoming painful event, not having choice may actually provide greater pain relief than having treatment choice. It is important to note that an additional pain dependent measure, the averaging of the concurrent pain reports, did not produce this same effect. Analysis of this measure revealed a significant interaction between the verbal expectation manipulation and prior experience but no effect of the choice manipulation. One possible explanation for this result stems from findings in earlier choice-placebo studies using the cold pressor paradigm. In these studies the initial pain reports were less sensitive to choice manipulations than were the later pain reports. As this aggregated pain measure combined early and later pain scores it may be less sensitive to the effects of choice (Rose et al., 2012).

The finding that prior experience moderates the influence of choice is consistent with research in the area of creative decision making. Specifically, research has found that individuals who possessed prior experience with a given task domain were the ones who benefited most from having choice between creativity tasks (Chua & Iyengar, 2008). Chua and Iyengar (2008) explained their results by suggesting that the individuals without prior experience were more likely to be overwhelmed and burdened by the choice event and thus failed to reap the benefits of choosing. The present results map on well with these earlier data.

Although prior experience can moderate the relationship between choice and placebo analgesia, it should not be anticipated that this moderation will always occur. Prior experience is likely a multifaceted construct, including one's knowledge, feelings, and learned behavior patterns. Given these complex underpinnings, its influence is likely to be fairly context-dependent. For example, the frequency and recency of the prior experience with the stimulus as well as the valence of this experience (positive or negative) should shape the impact of the prior experience. Further, other variables thought to alter placebo responding such as the strength of a placebo expectation and the desire for pain relief could also alter prior experience effects. Research on the role of prior stimulus experience and placebo analgesia is only now emerging and the findings of the present study suggest that clarifying prior experience effects will lead to a better understanding of pain relief.

Limitations

The present findings must be considered in light of a variety of limitations. One set of limitations concerns our use of a student sample as well as a laboratory pain task. Additional studies are required which focus on generalizability – testing the influence of prior pain stimulus exposure using clinical samples and a wide array of pain stimuli and events. Relatedly, our dependent measures consisted of self-reported pain and discomfort. The lack of other dependent variables, such as physiological measures, constrains the amount of information provided by this study. Finally, another notable limitation is that we measured prior experience and did not manipulate it. Consequently, it will be important for future studies to systematically manipulate prior stimulus experience to test the causal nature of this variable (Geers & Lassiter, 2005). It is worth mentioning, however, that even with this limitation the current study still indicates that assessing prior experience can be valuable in predicting how treatment choice affects placebo analgesia.

Implications

Taken together, the current findings coupled with those of the earlier placebo-choice studies have valuable implications for patient care. In particular, the data suggest that the current shift in medical care toward patient involvement may alter placebo analgesia and this can have costs or benefits for treatment outcomes. Specifically, it appears that involving individuals in treatment decision making can induce placebo analgesia in many cases. However, if individuals do not have prior experience with a pain modality – or the choice event for other reasons increases discomfort – placebo analgesia may not be strengthened by the provision of choice. If these results hold outside of the laboratory, health care practitioners could maximize patient outcomes by considering a patient's level of prior experience and adjust patient involvement accordingly. For example, if a health care practitioner knew that a patient has a long history of experiencing a specific kind of pain (e.g., migraines), the practitioner could give the patient greater involvement in the treatment decision making process to enhance placebo analgesia.

References

Botti, S., & Iyengar, S. S. (2004). The psychological pleasure and pain of choosing: When people prefer choosing at the cost of subsequent outcome satisfaction. *Journal of Personality and Social Psychology, 87*, 312–326.

Brown, J. A., Fowler, S. L., Rasinski, H. M., Rose, J. P., & Geers, A. L. (2013). Choice as a moderator of placebo expectation effects: Additional support from two experiments. *Basic and Applied Social Psychology, 35*, 436–444.
Calne, R., Calne, J., & Calne, S. (2009). Patient choice or patient abandoned? *Journal of Evaluation in Clinical Practice, 15*, 996–999.
Chua, R., & Iyengar, S. S. (2008). Creativity as a matter of choice: Prior experience and task instruction as boundary conditions for the positive effects of choice on creativity. *Journal of Creative Behavior, 42*, 164–180.
Colloca, L., & Benedetti, F. (2005). Placebos and painkillers: Is mind as real as matter? *Nature Reviews Neuroscience, 6*, 545–552.
Colloca, L., & Benedetti, F. (2006). How prior experience shapes placebo analgesia. *Pain, 124*, 126–133.
Hack, T. F., Degner, L. F., Watson, P., & Sinha, L. (2006). Do patients benefit from participating in medical decision making? Longitudinal follow-up of women with breast cancer. *Psycho-Oncology, 15*, 9–19.
Geers, A. L., & Lassiter, G. D. (2005). Affective assimilation and contrast: Effects of expectations and prior stimulus exposure. *Basic and Applied Social Psychology, 27*, 143–154.
Geers, A. L., & Rose, J. P. (2011). Treatment choice and placebo expectation effects. *Personality and Social Psychology Compass, 10*, 734–750.
Melzack, R. (1987). The short-form McGill pain questionnaire. *Pain, 30*(2), 191–197.
Rose, J. P., Geers, A. L., Rasinski, H. M., & Fowler, S. L. (2012). Treatment choice and pain analgesia. *Journal of Behavioral Medicine, 35*, 462–470.
Tracey, I. (2010). Getting the pain you expect: mechanisms of placebo, nocebo and reappraisal effects in humans. *Nature Medicine, 16*, 1277–1283.
Vase, L., Riley, J. L. III, & Price, D. D. (2002). A comparison of placebo effects in clinical analgesic trials versus studies of placebo analgesia. *Pain, 99*, 443–452.

Andrew L. Geers

Department of Psychology
University of Toledo
2801 West Bancroft St.
Toledo, OH 43606-3390
USA
Tel. +1 419 530-8530
Fax +1 419 530-8479
E-mail ageers@utnet.utoledo.edu

Original Article

Minimizing Carry-Over Effects After Treatment Failure and Maximizing Therapeutic Outcome

Can Changing the Route of Administration Mitigate the Influence of Treatment History?

Mareile Hofmann,[1,*] Nathalie Wrobel,[2,*] Simon Kessner,[3] and Ulrike Bingel[2]

[1]Schön Klinik, Bad Bramstedt, Germany, [2]Department of Neurology, University Hospital Essen, University Duisburg-Essen, Germany, [3]Department of Neurology, University Medical Center Hamburg-Eppendorf, Hamburg, Germany

Abstract. According to experimental and clinical evidence, the experiences of previous treatments are carried over to different therapeutic approaches and impair the outcome of subsequent treatments. In this behavioral pilot study we used a change in administration route to investigate whether the effect of prior treatment experience on a subsequent treatment depends on the similarity of both treatments. We experimentally induced positive or negative experiences with a topical analgesic treatment in two groups of healthy human subjects. Subsequently, we compared responses to a second, unrelated and systemic analgesic treatment between both the positive and negative group. We found that there was no difference in the analgesic response to the second treatment between the two groups. Our data indicate that a change in administration route might reduce the influence of treatment history and therefore be a way to reduce negative carry-over effects after treatment failure. Future studies will have to validate these findings in a fully balanced design including larger, clinical samples.

Keywords: placebo, pain, analgesia, behavioral conditioning

It has been a longstanding clinical notion that patients who have had negative experiences with a treatment tend to show reduced responses to subsequent treatment approaches. This phenomenon seems particularly evident in patients suffering from chronic diseases who often have a long treatment history. Experimental placebo analgesia studies involving a conditioning component have highlighted the pivotal role of treatment experiences on future treatment effects (Colloca & Benedetti, 2006; Montgomery & Kirsch, 1997; Voudouris, Peck, & Coleman, 1990; Wager et al., 2004). In these studies the administration of a placebo treatment is combined with a conditioning procedure (e.g., reduction of pain stimulus intensity) in which participants experience analgesia and thereby learn about the efficacy of the treatment. Subsequent responses to the same placebo treatment are substantially enhanced after this positive learning experience.

We have provided first experimental evidence that the influence of treatment experience on future treatment outcome is not limited to the same treatment approach (Kessner, Wiech, Forkmann, Ploner, & Bingel, 2013). In our study, we experimentally induced a positive or negative treatment experience with an analgesic treatment in two groups of healthy volunteers using a conditioning procedure. Subsequently, we compared how the two groups responded to a second, unrelated analgesic treatment. Based on behavioral and neurobiological evidence (fMRI) we were able to show that the experience with one treatment substantially modulates the response to a second, unrelated analgesic treatment. Our findings therefore substantiate observations from pharmacological cross-over studies (i.e., drug trials in which subjects receive an active drug and a placebo in a randomized order) which had suggested a "carry-over" of treatment effects from placebo to active treatments, from active treatments to placebo, and between two different active treatments (André-Obadia, Magnin, & Garcia-Larrea, 2011; Batterman & Lower, 1968; Suchman & Ader, 1992). From a learning perspective this illustrates that not only particular aspects of a treatment (e.g., shape and taste of a pill) can serve as the conditioned stimulus, but that the entire treatment context can trigger learned responses.

* Both authors contributed equally to this manuscript.

DOI: 10.1027/2151-2604/a000180

Given that treatment experiences are ubiquitous in clinical care, these findings have important implications for medical practice and clinical trial design. Carry-over effects might be particularly relevant in chronic conditions in which treatments often fail repetitively. Importantly, the negative treatment experiences which accumulate along the course of the disease are also likely to hamper the response to otherwise potent treatments. It would therefore be desirable to systematically target carry-over effects, that is, to reduce the influence of treatment experience on consecutive treatments in case of prior treatment failure or to enhance it in the case of treatment success.

In our previous study two locally applied "treatments" (i.e., a patch and an ointment) with presumably different pharmacological profiles were employed. According to the conditioning literature (Shepard, 1987) carry-over effects are stronger the more similar the conditioned stimuli are in appearance. If this holds true for learning effects in drug treatments, a change in application route should minimize negative carry-over effects after treatment failure. In this behavioral pilot study, we investigated whether the effect of prior treatment experience on a subsequent treatment approach depends on the similarity of both treatments. We used an established experimental model (Kessner et al., 2013) that allows for the assessment of treatment history effects on future treatment outcomes, irrespective of pharmacological peculiarities, in order to investigate whether a change in application route affects the carry-over effect of two subsequent treatments. As in our prior study, we experimentally induced positive or negative treatment history in two groups of healthy human subjects by combining a locally applied placebo treatment (inert patch) and a conditioning procedure. Subsequently we changed the application route from topical application (patch) to systemically applied treatment (pill) and compared the analgesic responses between the positive and negative treatment experience group.

We hypothesized that a change in application route would reduce the carry-over effect between treatment approaches. More specifically, we expected that the efficacy of the subsequent treatment would be less affected by the treatment experience with a prior treatment if the application route differed between both treatments.

Materials and Methods

Subjects

Thirty healthy volunteers (mean age: 25.2 years, range: 19–36; 16 females) participated in this study and were randomly assigned to either the positive or negative treatment experience group. The groups did not differ significantly with respect to age, gender, or several psychological scores that might influence the individual effect of prior treatment experiences (i.e., depression, anxiety, beliefs about medicine; see participants' characteristics in Table 1). None of the participants were taking any medication except for oral contraceptives or thyroid medication. During recruitment, participants were told to refrain from taking any pain medication 24 hr before entering the trial.

Participants were informed that the purpose of the study was to investigate inter-individual differences in the efficacy of analgesics. Furthermore, participants were told that both treatments (day 1 & 2 and day 3) were effective painkillers for local heat pain and examples of indications and clinical use were explained to each participant.

All subjects had heat pain thresholds in a normal range at the site of stimulation (see Results) and had no known history of neurological or psychiatric diseases, including recurrent or chronic pain. The study was approved by the local Ethics Committee of the Medical Board in Hamburg, Germany and all experimental procedures conformed to the Declaration of Helsinki. All participants gave written informed consent to the experimental procedures and were free to withdraw from the study at any time.

Table 1. Participants' demographics and questionnaire results

	Negative treatment history group	Positive treatment history group	
N	15	15	30
Age	25.6 ± 4.6	24.9 ± 4.8	25.2 ± 4.6
Gender			
Woman	8	8	16
Man	7	7	14
Center for Epidemiological Studies Depression Scale	8.6 ± 6.3	8.9 ± 7.6	$t(28) = -0.130$ n.s.
State-Trait Anxiety Inventory			
State	32.7 ± 7.5	33.0 ± 8.6	$t(28) = -0.090$ n.s.
Trait	31.4 ± 8.5	34.3 ± 8.5	$t(28) = -0.921$ n.s.
Beliefs about Medicines Questionnaire			
Specific-Necessity	17.6 ± 2.1	16.7 ± 3.4	$t(28) = 0.903$ n.s.
Specific-Concerns	24.9 ± 4.9	26.6 ± 3.2	$t(28) = -1.090$ n.s.
General-Overuse	10.4 ± 2.1	10.5 ± 2.0	$t(28) = -0.177$ n.s.
General-Harm	13.9 ± 2.2	14.3 ± 2.0	$t(28) = -0.438$ n.s.

Experimental Paradigm

We used a 2 × 2 mixed-factorial design with the between-subject factor treatment history (*negative vs. positive*) and the within-subject factor treatment site (*treated vs. untreated site*) as previously described in Kessner et al. (2013). In the following, the term "untreated" site will refer to the stimulation site before treatment and "treated" site will be used for the site stimulated after treatment (patch/or pill), as in our previous publication Kessner et al. (2013).

Experimental Procedures

The experiment took place on three consecutive days. In a first *conditioning phase* (day 1 and 2) the positive or negative treatment experience was induced by an inert patch treatment (local application) combined with a conditioning procedure (Voudouris, Peck, & Coleman, 1985). During the *test phase* performed on day 3 the analgesic response to a second analgesic treatment was assessed through self-report. To make the second treatment sufficiently different from the first treatment, the second treatment was delivered as an oral systemic treatment (pill) in contrast to the locally applied patch.

Conditioning Phase (Days 1 and 2)

Upon arrival for the first session, subjects were informed about the experimental procedures and written informed consent was obtained. All instructions were read to the participants to ensure a standardized procedure. For the noxious stimulation tonic, heat stimuli were applied to the skin of the left inner forearm by attaching a thermode (30 × 30 mm^2 ATS thermode, Pathway system, Medoc, Israel). First, we determined the individual heat pain threshold using the Method of Limits (Fruhstorfer, Lindblom, & Schmidt, 1976).

Subsequently, participants were familiarized with the equipment and rating procedure. For this purpose, several stimuli of different temperature levels were applied to the left forearm. Participants were asked to rate on a visual analog scale (VAS, [100 parts; endpoints labeled as "no pain" and "unbearable pain"]). Second, a temperature calibration was performed to determine the individual temperatures evoking pain levels of 20, 50, and 80 on the VAS. To this end, a pseudo-randomized sequence of twelve 20 s thermal stimuli of different temperature levels was applied. Participants were instructed to rate the intensity of each stimulus on the VAS. Based on these ratings, stimulation intensities corresponding to subjective pain intensity ratings of VAS 20, 50, and 80 were determined by means of regression analysis to ensure a perception-locked stimulation across subjects. This procedure was repeated on day 2.

Before the conditioning phase commenced, subjects had to indicate how effectively they expect the "analgesic patch" to reduce pain (on a VAS from 0 [no pain reduction] to 10 [extremely strong pain reduction]). Next, a negative or positive treatment history was induced by a conditioning procedure. To this end, an inert skin patch (treatment A) was applied to the left forearm (see Figure 1). The 7 × 5 cm^2 patch consisted of a white cotton tissue with an inert sticky layer that was attached to the skin and removed after 20 min. During the actual conditioning session, a series of 20 heat pain stimuli (duration 20 s, interstimulus interval 40 s) was applied to the treated or the untreated site, which was several cm next to the patch treated site, in randomized order. The intensity of the stimuli on the treated site differed between subjects depending on the assignment to the "negative" or the "positive" treatment history group. In the positive treatment history group, a low stimulation intensity (corresponding to a VAS pain rating of 20) was applied to the patch treated site to mimic analgesia while an intensity of VAS 80 was applied to the untreated site. This manipulation was unbeknownst to the participants. In contrast, the negative treatment history group received the same stimulation intensity of VAS 80 on the untreated and the treated site. In order to reinforce the positive or negative drug experience with the patch, this conditioning procedure was performed twice and thus repeated on two consecutive days in both groups. After the stimulation procedure participants were asked to rate the analgesic efficacy of the used patch on a numerical analog scale [NAS from 0 [no pain reduction] to 5 [extremely strong pain reduction].

Test Phase (Day 3)

The test phase was identical for both groups. On day 3, the positive and negative treatment history groups were instructed that another analgesic with a different pharmacological profile would be administered as an oral pill. Importantly, to ensure that participants hold similar expectations of the two different routes of application used in the study, we assessed pretreatment expectations of the analgesic efficacy in a different cohort of healthy participants (see Preliminary study). This pilot study confirmed pill and patch as not being perceived significantly different in efficacy when used as analgesics for pain relief of heat pain stimuli.

The test phase commenced by determining the individual pain threshold. Next, 15 heat pain stimuli of a high intensity (VAS 80) were applied to the untreated site. Participants then received the second treatment that differed from the first treatment used on day 1 and 2 in application route. For that, a pill without an active ingredient was delivered as a systemic treatment in contrast to the locally applied placebo patch that was used during the conditioning phase. During a waiting period of 45 min, in which the "pill should become effective," participants had to fill in several questionnaires (see Questionnaires). Next, we applied 15 heat pain stimuli of a reduced intensity corresponding to a VAS 50 on the treated site to all participants irrespective of the group to mimic the analgesic effect of the pill treatment.

Participants rated the intensity of each stimulus on a VAS. We hypothesized a difference of the analgesic effect of the second treatment on the treated site on day 3 between both groups. All our manipulations were unbeknownst to

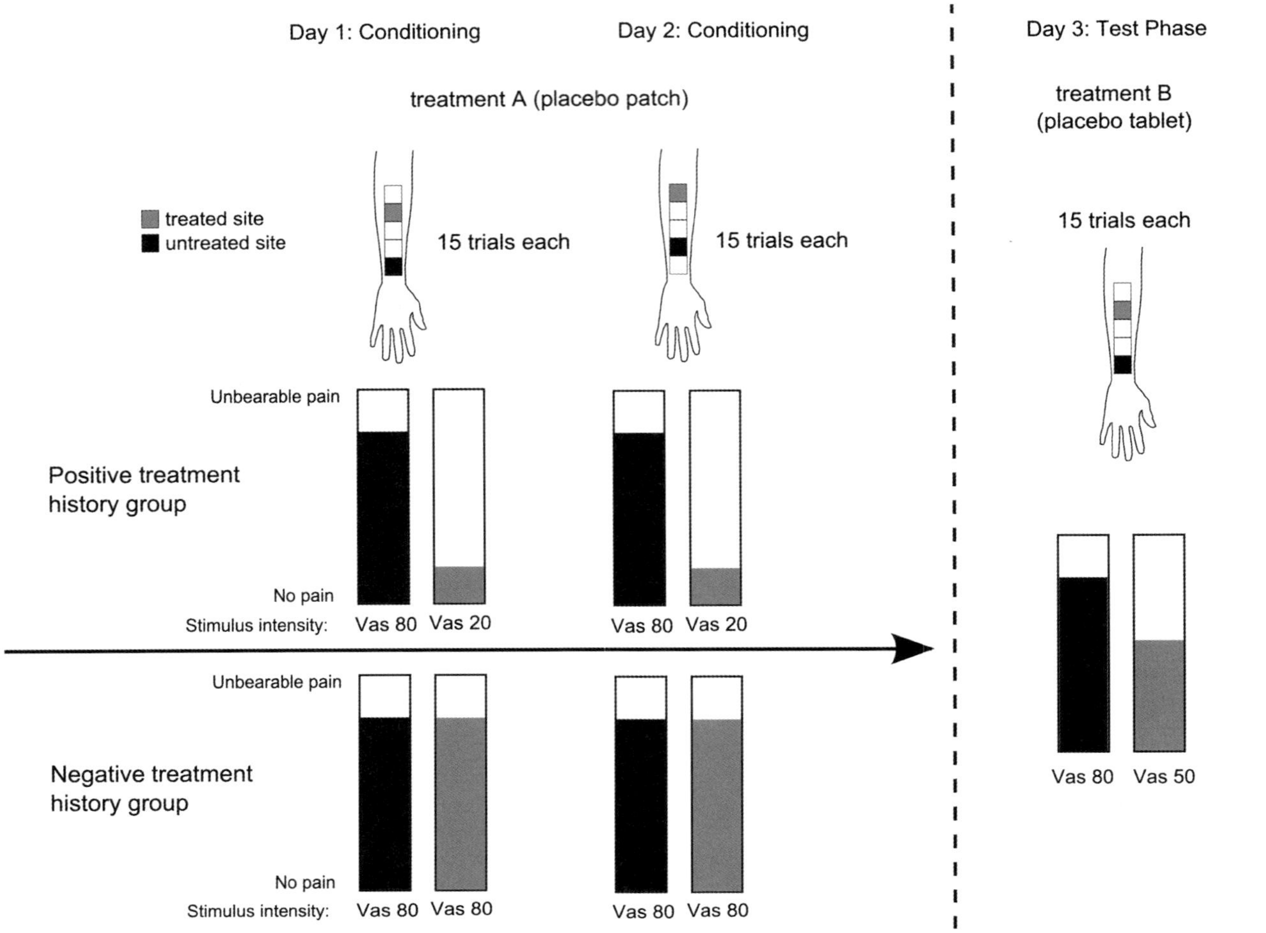

Figure 1. Experimental design. The experiment took place on three consecutive days. Volunteers were randomized into two groups to experimentally induce either a positive or negative treatment experience with a first treatment A (inert patch) introduced as analgesic. Treatment experiences were induced by a stimulus intensity manipulation that was unbeknownst to the participant. In the positive treatment history group stimulation intensities were reduced to VAS 20 following the "analgesic" treatment, whereas in the negative treatment history group the stimulation intensity of VAS 80 was applied. The conditioning procedure consisted of 15 heat stimuli (duration 20 s) applied on the treated and untreated site on two consecutive days, respectively. The test phase on day 3 was identical for both groups. Participants were instructed that another analgesic with a different pharmacological profile would be administered. 15 heat stimuli with the intensity VAS 80 were applied to the untreated site of the participants' left forearm. Next an inert white pill (treatment B) was taken and after a waiting period 15 heat stimuli with the intensity of VAS 50 were applied to the treated site. Again, the analgesic treatment was modeled experimentally by reducing the stimulus intensity to VAS 50 for the treatment session. The analgesic response to the second analgesic treatment was compared between the positive and negative treatment history group.

the participants. At the end of the test session, participants rated the analgesic efficacy of the pill on a NAS as previously described in the conditioning phase.

This rigid order of the experimental conditions (untreated site in first session and "treated site" in the second session following oral analgesic treatment) had to be performed due to the change of the supposedly analgesic application route from local to systemic. Participants were informed that due to the systemic application of the analgesic treatment, eliminating the drug would have taken several hours and would therefore have confounded the results for the untreated site. As confirmed by pilot data and previous studies (Kessner et al., 2013) the stimulation protocol used in this study did not evoke any significant time dependent effects (such as sensitization or habituation) that would possibly confound the results of a fixed order regimen.

Pilot Study

As we were specifically interested in the effect of a change in application route on the carry-over effect of treatment experiences, but not main effects of different application forms, it was crucial that the two different routes of application used in our study would not evoke different analgesic expectations that could confound the treatment response in the test session. To identify two routes of application that induce most similar analgesic treatment expectations we investigated healthy participants' pretreatment expectations of different application forms in a pilot study and compared expectation ratings of the application route "patch" used in our main study with five different other application routes. Fifty volunteers rated the expected efficacy of a patch, ointment, pill, nasal spray, chewable tablet, and drops to alleviate pain induced by thermal stimuli applied to the forearm on a VAS [from 0 "no pain reduction" to 10 "complete pain reduction"]. A repeated measures ANOVA and five post hoc *t*-tests were used to analyze the results (Bonferroni-corrected $\alpha = 0.01$; mean ratings ± *SD*). The main effect of expectation was $F_{(3,123)} = 19.2, p < .001$, indicating different expectancies concerning the effectives of the different medication forms. To follow up and determine a medication "pair" with similar expectancies, we compared the patch and every other medication form pairwise performing post hoc *t*-tests. The expectation of pain relief from pill and patch (mean pill: 42.3 VAS ± 24.5 VAS; mean patch: 51.3 VAS ± 22.3 VAS, $t_{(49)} = 1.74$; $p = .088$) and patch and drops (mean drops: 41.6 VAS ± 2.8 VAS, $t_{(49)} = 1.98$; $p = .052$) did not differ significantly. (Other pairs: patch/ointment $t_{(49)} = -3.66$, $p = .001$; patch/chewable tablet $t_{(49)} = 3.41$, $p = .001$; Patch/nasal spray $t_{(49)} = 5.76$, $p < .001$). Based on these findings we decided to use a patch for the first treatment and a pill for the second treatment.

Questionnaires

To assess psychological trait variables, beliefs and treatment experiences that could affect conditioning and carry-over, validated questionnaires were used. These include the German version of the Beliefs about medicines questionnaire: BMQ-D (Horne, Weinman, & Hankins, 1999), the State Trait Anxiety Inventory (STAI; Spielberger, 1983), the Center for Epidemiologic Studies – Depression Scale (CES-D; Radloff, 1977); German version: ADS-K, (Hautzinger & Bailer, 1993). *T*-tests were used to ensure the groups did not differ with respect to scores (see Table 1).

Analysis of Self-Report

VAS ratings were recorded by the stimulation program Presentation® and analyzed using SPSS 18.0.

The main outcome measure was the analgesic effect of the treatment condition on the test day. This was defined as the difference in pain-related ratings between the treated and the untreated site on day 3. The difference of this analgesic effect between both treatment history groups on day 3 was analyzed with a mixed two-way analysis of variances (ANOVA), with the between-subject factor treatment history group (positive vs. negative) and the within-subject factor treatment site (treated vs. untreated site). Unless otherwise specified, results with a $p < .05$ are considered statistically significant. As additional outcome measures, pain thresholds and expected effectiveness ratings during the two conditioning sessions were analyzed using repeated ANOVAs. The conditioning data was analyzed using a $2 \times 2 \times 2$ repeated measures ANOVA with time (day 1 vs. day 2) as an additional factor followed by 2 post hoc *t*-tests.

We also analyzed the experienced efficacy of the analgesic cream on the 3 days (3 Mann-Whitney U tests). *T*-tests were used to compare the expected pain relief on day 2 and 3 as well as the temperatures applied in untreated and treated conditions on day 3.

Results

Pain Thresholds and Pain Sensitivity

All volunteers showed mean pain thresholds in the normal range (Rolke et al., 2006, positive treatment history group 46.7 °C ± 1.6 °C; negative treatment history group 45.72 °C ± 2.2 °C). Pain thresholds on days 1–3 did not differ between both treatment history – groups (main effect treatment history group: $F_{(1,28)} = 2.5, p = .125$). There was no main effect of time ($F_{(1,35)} = 1.891, p = .177$) as well as no interaction effect of time/treatment history group ($F_{(1,28)} = 0.742$, $p = .396$), indicating a stable threshold without group differences over time.

To ensure that the heat stimuli were physically identical for both treatment history groups on day 3, we compared the temperatures applied in both groups for the untreated and treated site. Temperatures did not differ between the untreated or treated site respectively (untreated site positive treatment history group 47.1 °C ± 0.7 °C, negative treatment history group 46.9 °C ± 0.7 °C, $t_{(28)} = -0.982$, $p = .880$; treated site positive treatment history group 46.3 °C ± 0.8 °C, negative treatment history group 45.8 °C ± 0.8 °C, $t_{(28)} = -1.36$, $p = .184$).

Conditioning

Pain ratings reveal that treated and untreated sites were rated significantly different across treatment history group and treatment site thus confirming a successful manipulation of the pain experience (interaction treatment history group-by-treatment site: $F_{(1,28)} = 218.9$, $p < .001$, main effect treatment site: $F_{(1,28)} = 243.8$, $p < .001$, main effect of treatment history group: $F_{(1,28)} = 77.7, p < 0.001$). There was no effect of time ($F_{(1,28)} = 0.0, p = .837$) as well as no other significant interaction (time-by-treatment history group interaction: $F_{(1,28)} = 2.4$, $p = .134$; treatment site-by-time interaction: $F_{(1,28)} = 0.9$, $p = .344$; treatment

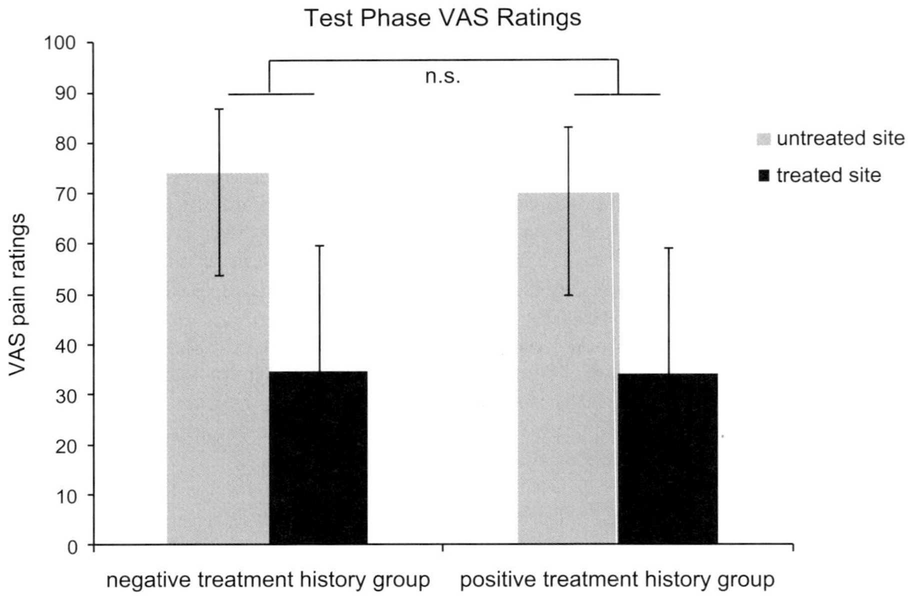

Figure 2. Results of the test phase/day 3. According to the temperature manipulation on day 3 (reduction from VAS 80 to 50 on the treated site), subject's ratings on the treated site were lower compared to the untreated site. Pain ratings (VAS ratings ± SEM) indicate that the therapeutic effect of the systemic pill treatment (treatment B) did not differ significantly between the negative and the positive treatment history group after manipulation of treatment experiences on day 1–2 and the change of application route on day 3.

site-by-time-by-treatment history group: $F_{(1,28)} = 0.1$, $p = .744$).

Post hoc *t*-tests comparing the average pain rating of the treatment site between the groups reveal a significant difference of the treated site but not the untreated site, confirming the treatment history group manipulation and indicating that the conditioning procedure was successful (positive treatment history group: treated site: 16.1 ± 12.2 VAS; untreated site: 74.6 ± 11.3 VAS; negative treatment history group: treated site: 73.5 ± 10.2 VAS; untreated site: 75.0 ± 12.5 VAS; untreated site: $t_{(28)} = 15.1$, $p < .001$; treated site: $t_{(28)} = 0.1$, $p = .94$).

Expectation and Perceived Efficacy During the Conditioning Phase

These findings were confirmed by the participants' judgments of expected and perceived efficacy. On day 2, the positive treatment history group expected a greater pain relief from the patch than the negative treatment history group (negative treatment history group 11.7 VAS ± 11.9 VAS, positive treatment history group 75.7 VAS ± 20.5 VAS, $t_{(28)} = -10.48$, $p < .001$). Accordingly, the ratings of efficacy after treatment on day 1 and 2 differed significantly between the positive and the negative treatment history group (day 1: $U = 1.5$, $Z = -4.7$, $p < .001$; day 2: $U = 3.5$, $Z = -4.6$, $p < .001$).

Test Phase

In line with our temperature manipulation on day 3 (reduction from VAS 80 to 50 on the treated site), subject's ratings on the treated site were significantly lower compared to the untreated site (negative treatment history group: treated site 34.6 VAS ± 11.4, untreated site 74 VAS ± 9.1; positive treatment history group: treated site 34.1 VAS ± 13.6, untreated site 69.9 VAS ± 14.9; main effect of treatment site: $F_{(1,28)} = 150.1$, $p < .001$). There was no main effect of treatment history group ($F_{(1,28)} = 0.468$, $p = .5$). Importantly, the treatment history group-by-treatment site interaction was not statistically significant ($F_{(1,28)} = 0.33$, $p = .57$), indicating no significant "carry-over" of treatment experience from the patch to the oral analgesic treatment, as illustrated in Figure 2 (ΔVAS day 3: positive treatment history group: ΔVAS = 35.77; negative treatment history group: ΔVAS = 39.3; positive treatment history group: 34.1 ± 13.6 VAS on the treated site and 69.9 ± 14.9 VAS on the untreated site; negative treatment history group: 34.6 ± 1.3 VAS on the treated site and 73.9 ± 9.1 VAS on the untreated site).

As intended, expectations of the analgesic benefit from the second treatment did not differ significantly between the treatment history groups (negative treatment history group: 61.7 VAS ± 17.1 VAS; positive treatment history group: 58.6 VAS ± 21.9 VAS; $t_{(28)} = 0.437$, $p = .665$).

Unexpectedly, after completion of the stimulation session, participants of the negative treatment history group even rated the second analgesic treatment as significantly more effective than the positive treatment history group (median negative treatment history group = 4, median positive treatment history group = 3, $U = 61$, $Z = -2.21$, $p = .026$).

Discussion

In this study we investigated whether the effect of prior treatment experience on a subsequent treatment approach depends on the similarity of both treatments. We systematically varied one important variable of the treatment context between two subsequent treatments, namely the route of administration which was changed from a topical to a systemic application.

We used an established experimental model of analgesia (Kessner et al., 2013) that allows for the assessment of a treatment history effect on future treatment outcomes irrespective of pharmacological peculiarities in order to investigate if a change in the route of administration modulates the carry-over effect of two subsequent treatments. As in our previous study, we experimentally induced positive or negative treatment experience in two groups of healthy human subjects by combining a locally applied placebo treatment (inert patch) and a conditioning procedure. We subsequently changed the route of administration of the (supposedly) analgesic treatment from an analgesic patch (topical application) to an analgesic pill (systemic treatment) and compared the analgesic responses between the positive and negative treatment history group.

In contrast to our previous study (Kessner et al., 2013), no statistically significant differences were found between the two groups with different treatment experience. Overall, participants showed the same analgesic response to the second, systemic treatment (pill) regardless of their previous positive or negative treatment history with the local treatment (patch). These findings indicate that the "outcome" of the first treatment did not affect the two subsequent treatments which varied substantially in their application route. From a clinical point of view these behavioral data support the notion that changing the route of administration of a treatment might be a promising way to overcome negative carry-over effects.

While the effect of expectancy on treatment outcomes has previously attracted attention and has been investigated in various studies (Bausell, Lao, Bergman, Lee, & Berman, 2005; Bingel et al., 2011; Colloca, Lopiano, Lanotte, & Benedetti, 2004; Linde et al., 2007; Pollo et al., 2001), (pharmaco)therapy is only rarely considered from a learning perspective although both experimental and clinical evidence indicate that learning mechanisms (e.g., behavioral conditioning) can modify treatment responses considerably and might contribute to insufficient treatment responses, particularly in the context of prior treatment failures.

Our previous study has provided strong behavioral and neuroimaging evidence for a carry-over effect between two similar locally applied analgesic treatments (patch and ointment). Participants with an experimentally induced negative experience with the first treatment also showed a substantially reduced response to a second analgesic treatment (Kessner et al., 2013).

Based on these findings, the aim of this behavioral pilot study was to explore if this potentially detrimental carry-over effect of negative treatment experiences on subsequent treatments can be reduced by a change in application route between treatments. As predicted by findings from the conditioning literature which suggests that "carry-over effects" are stronger the more similar the conditioned stimuli are in appearance (Shepard, 1987), we observed no significant carry-over effect between the two treatments with very dissimilar application routes. We thereby provide evidence that carry-over effects after treatment failure might be reduced by a change in application route. These findings might motivate approaches to systematically vary the application route of treatments based on patients' treatment experiences beyond pharmacodynamical considerations, as currently done in pharmacotherapy. Such approaches might be particularly beneficial for patients suffering from chronic diseases. Here, treatment applications could be varied systematically to reduce the negative effects of earlier treatment failure, or remain unaltered in case of sufficient prior treatment responses to optimize overall treatment outcome. The same strategies might be applied to modulate the impact of prior unwanted side effects, although our study did not address this aspect specifically.

However, these preliminary findings have to be seen in the light of several limitations that have to be addressed in future investigations. Due to the small sample size, we did not include a control group in which the same application route was used across all three treatment days instead of switching the route of administration as was done in this study. The main conclusion from our study, namely that changing the application route reduces the carry-over effect is therefore based on the comparison with our previous study, which was performed using the same experimental procedures and setting. However, this sequential study approach also involved a change in the main investigator, which was male in the previous study and female in the current study. This change in the main experimenter/investigator might compromise the comparability of the two studies and we cannot exclude that this change has affected the effect of treatment change on treatment outcome.

Together with our previous study these current findings further support the notion that treatment responses are not solely determined by pharmacological properties of a treatment, but are substantially modulated by the treatment context including learning mechanisms. Our study thereby provides promising first evidence that a systematic consideration and potential modulation of aspects of the treatment context might improve treatment outcomes and emphasizes the importance of a careful assessment of prior treatment history before switching to a different treatment.

Acknowledgments

This work was supported by grants from the German Research Foundation (DFG FOR-1329) and the Federal Ministry of Education and Research (01GQ0808). We thank Katharina Schmidt and Odette Schunke for support.

References

André-Obadia, N., Magnin, M., & Garcia-Larrea, L. (2011). On the importance of placebo timing in rTMS studies for pain relief. *Pain, 152*, 1233–1237. doi: 10.1016/j.pain.2010.12.027

Batterman, R. C., & Lower, W. R. (1968). Placebo responsiveness – influence of previous therapy. *Current Therapeutic Research, Clinical and Experimental, 10*, 136–143.

Bausell, R. B., Lao, L., Bergman, S., Lee, W. L., & Berman, B. M. (2005). Is acupuncture analgesia an expectancy effect? Preliminary evidence based on participants' perceived assignments in two placebo-controlled trials. *Evaluation & the Health Professions, 28*, 9–26. doi: 10.1177/0163278704273081

Bingel, U., Wanigasekera, V., Wiech, K., Ni Mhuircheartaigh, R., Lee, M. C., Ploner, M., & Tracey, I. (2011). The effect of treatment expectation on drug efficacy: Imaging the analgesic benefit of the opioid remifentanil. *Science Translational Medicine, 3*, 70ra14. doi: 10.1126/scitranslmed.3001244

Colloca, L., & Benedetti, F. (2006). How prior experience shapes placebo analgesia. *Pain, 124*, 126–133. doi: 10.1016/j.pain.2006.04.005

Colloca, L., Lopiano, L., Lanotte, M., & Benedetti, F. (2004). Overt versus covert treatment for pain, anxiety, and Parkinson's disease. *Lancet Neurology, 3*, 679–684. doi: 10.1016/S1474-4422(04)00908-1

Fruhstorfer, H., Lindblom, U., & Schmidt, W. C. (1976). Method for quantitative estimation of thermal thresholds in patients. *Journal of Neurology, Neurosurgergy, and Psychiatry, 39*, 1071–1075.

Hautzinger, M., & Bailer, M. (1993). *ADS Allgemeine Depressionsskala* [General depression scale]. Göttingen, Germany: Beltz Test.

Horne, R., Weinman, J., & Hankins, M. (1999). The beliefs about medicines questionnaire: The development and evaluation of a new method for assessing the cognitive representation of medication. *Psychology & Health, 14*(1), 1–24. doi: 10.1080/08870449908407311

Kessner, S., Wiech, K., Forkmann, K., Ploner, M., & Bingel, U. (2013). The effect of treatment history on therapeutic outcome: An experimental approach. *JAMA Internal Medicine, 173*, 1468–1469. doi: 10.1001/jamainternmed.2013.6705

Linde, K., Witt, C. M., Streng, A., Weidenhammer, W., Wagenpfeil, S., Brinkhaus, B., ... Melchart, D. (2007). The impact of patient expectations on outcomes in four randomized controlled trials of acupuncture in patients with chronic pain. *Pain, 128*, 264–271. doi: 10.1016/j.pain.2006.12.006

Montgomery, G. H., & Kirsch, I. (1997). Classical conditioning and the placebo effect. *Pain, 72*, 107–113.

Pollo, A., Amanzio, M., Arslanian, A., Casadio, C., Maggi, G., & Benedetti, F. (2001). Response expectancies in placebo analgesia and their clinical relevance. *Pain, 93*, 77–84.

Radloff, L. S. (1977). The CES-D scale a self-report depression scale for research in the general population. *Applied Psychological Measurement, 1*, 385–401.

Shepard, R. N. (1987). Toward a universal law of generalization for psychological science. *Science, 237*, 1317–1323.

Spielberger, C. (1983). Foreword [Special Issue: Behavioral Medicine]. *International Review of Applied Psychology – Revue Internationale De Psychologie Appliquee, 32*, 1–4.

Suchman, A. L., & Ader, R. (1992). Classic conditioning and placebo effects in crossover studies. *Clinical Pharmacology and Therapeutics, 52*, 372–377.

Voudouris, N. J., Peck, C. L., & Coleman, G. (1985). Conditioned placebo responses. *Journal of Personality and Social Psychology, 48*, 47–53.

Voudouris, N. J., Peck, C. L., & Coleman, G. (1990). The role of conditioning and verbal expectancy in the placebo response. *Pain, 43*, 121–128.

Wager, T. D., Rilling, J. K., Smith, E. E., Sokolik, A., Casey, K. L., Davidson, R. J., ... Cohen, J. D. (2004). Placebo-induced changes in fMRI in the anticipation and experience of pain. *Science, 303*, 1162–1167. doi: 10.1126/science.1093065

Ulrike Bingel

Clinic for Neurology
University Clinic Essen
Hufelandstr. 55
45122 Essen
Germany
Tel. +49 201 723-2165
E-mail ulrike.bingel@uk-essen.de

Original Article

Analgesics in Chronic Back Pain

The Significance of Patient Attitudes to Them and Prior Experience With Them for Placebo Responses

Sandra Kamping,[1] Maike Müller,[1] Regine Klinger,[2] Julia Schmitz,[2] and Herta Flor[1]

[1]Department of Cognitive and Clinical Neuroscience, Central Institute of Mental Health, Medical Faculty Mannheim, Heidelberg University, Germany, [2]Psychotherapeutic Outpatient Clinic Behavior Therapy, Department of Psychology, University of Hamburg, Germany

Abstract. Patients' attitude toward and their personal experience of analgesics may not only influence their expectations about new medications they are prescribed but might also influence placebo effects. We assessed attitudes toward pain medication with an 8-item instrument and experiences with pain medication with an 11-item instrument and evaluated the relationship of attitudes and experiences and placebo responses in chronic back pain patients. On average, patients reported a slightly negative attitude toward analgesics and a slightly positive experience with them compared to healthy pain-free controls that had a more positive attitude toward and experience of analgesics. Pain patients seemed to report their short-term experience with analgesics when completing our instrument, as can be seen by the regression of experience with pain medication and the subscale short-term efficacy of non-/minimally invasive pain medication of the pain interview. Using a pharmacological placebo in a subsample of 38 patients, we were able to show that patients with positive attitudes had a larger placebo response than patients with negative attitudes. The size of the placebo response could be predicted using the mean attitude score. Future placebo research assessing patients' attitudes toward analgesics seems important and could help to understand the results obtained.

Keywords: chronic back pain, attitude, experience, pain medication, placebo response

Placebo analgesia describes the reduction of pain after the application of a pharmacologically inactive substance. A large number of studies have shown that placebo analgesia is based on two major factors: expectation and classical conditioning (Voudouris, Peck, & Coleman, 1990). Additionally, psychosocial factors, like the interaction between therapist and patient and attitude toward a treatment are important in the development and strengthening of the placebo effect. These factors, together with prior experience (Finniss, Kaptchuk, Miller, & Benedetti, 2010) and expectation of treatment success (Pollo & Benedetti, 2009), seem to be pivotal in placebo analgesia. Colloca and Benedetti (2006) manipulated the prior experience of healthy subjects by attaching a sham electrode and giving the verbal instruction that a green light would precede the activation of the electrode, which would induce an analgesic effect. A preceding red light would mean that the electrode was not activated and no analgesic effect would be present. For one group of subjects this verbal instruction was correct, that is, the stimulation intensity following the green light was reduced below pain threshold and for another group the painful stimuli following either light were above pain threshold. In a control trial at the end they administered painful stimuli under the green and red light conditions to measure the size of the placebo effect elicited by the green light. They showed that the size of the placebo effect that their healthy participants developed was dependent on the prior experience they had in the experimental session. Subjects with a positive prior experience (pain reduction) showed larger placebo effects than subjects with a negative prior experience (where pain was not reduced).

Chronic pain patients who use analgesic treatments may have varying experiences and attitudes about their efficacy and this may influence their response to placebos. However, this relationship has not been examined in a systematic manner. Research on attitudes toward medication in patients in general has commonly employed two questionnaires. The Beliefs about Medicines Questionnaire (BMQ; Horne, Weinmann, & Hankins, 1999) consists of 28 questions and measures attitudes toward medicines in general (BMQ General) with the subscales "perceived overuse of medicines by doctors" and "harmfulness of medication" and attitudes toward medications that are used by the patient (BMQ Specific) with the subscales "necessity" and "concerns." The Pain Medication Attitude Questionnaire (PMAQ; McCracken, Hoskins, & Eccleston, 2006) consists of 47 items and assesses different concerns and views pain patients have about medication intake with the subscales addiction, perceived need, unfavorable scrutiny by others, adverse side effects, tolerance, mistrust in the prescribing doctor, and withdrawal. No specific instrument about attitudes and experiences with analgesics has been developed.

DOI: 10.1027/2151-2604/a000182

The aim of the present study was to use a short instrument that captures patients' attitude toward and their experience with pain medication. Additionally, we examined the relationship of attitude and experience with the size of patients' placebo response. We expected that pain patients' attitudes toward pain medication might be slightly negative (i.e., not helping them with their pain in the long run), whereas it should be more positive for control subjects. We also expected patients' ratings of their experience with pain medication as more negative (i.e., many unsuccessful therapeutic interventions), compared to pain-free control subjects who should rate their experience with pain medication as more positive. Finally, we expected placebo effects to be larger with more positive attitudes and experiences.

Materials and Methods

Participants

One-hundred-and-one patients with unspecific chronic back pain in two study centers (68 in Mannheim, 33 in Hamburg) completed a scale on pain-related attitudes and a scale on pain-related experiences (see below). The patients were on average 52.16 years old (*SD* = 13.63, range = 18–73), 47 were female, 54 male, and the average time they had spent in education was 10.83 years (*SD* = 1.83, range = 8–15). They reported a mean total pain duration of 11.53 years (*SD* = 11.80, range = 0.83–60 years). The mean pain intensity (as measured with the German version of the West-Haven Yale Multidimensional Pain Inventory (Flor, Rudy, Birbaumer, Streit, & Schugens, 1990)) was 3.11 (*SD* = 1.13, range = 0.67–5.67) and the mean interference with pain was 2.96 (*SD* = 1.33, range = 0.20–5.90; see Table 1 for further characteristics of the study sample). Exclusion criteria were inflammatory or neurological disorders, intake of opioid medication and major mental disorder. Additionally, 25 healthy pain-free control subjects were evaluated (mean age = 52.12, *SD* = 12.00, range = 22–70; 17 male).

Assessment

The patients' attitude related to analgesic medication was assessed with an eight-item instrument. The attitude scales took the patients' own experience with medication into account and consisted of the following options:

(1) Pain medication helps me to live a better life.
(2) I am willing to put up with the side effects of pain medication, if this makes me feel better.
(3) As soon as I feel better I discontinue my pain medication.
(4) It is not healthy for me and my body to take pain medication.
(5) Generally, I do not have problems taking pain medication.
(6) I tend to bear my pain instead of taking pain medication.
(7) When I am in pain I take my pain medication immediately.
(8) Generally, I do not like to take pain medication.

The scale ranged from 1 = do not agree at all, 2 = somewhat disagree, 3 = somewhat agree, to 4 = agree fully.

Items 1, 4, 5, 7, and 9 needed to be recoded in order to achieve a unified rating. The overall score was constructed as the mean of the individual eight items. The minimum score a subject could obtain was 1 = very negative attitude toward medication, the maximum score was 4 = very positive attitude toward medication.

The patients' experience with analgesic medication was assessed with an 11-item instrument. The 11 questions consisted of three sections. Patients were asked whether they had taken a specific medication (yes or no) and then to rate the efficacy of this specific medication in alleviating their

Table 1. Patient characteristics

	Number of patients	Mean	Standard deviation	Range
Age	100	52.16	13.63	18.00–73.00
Sex	101		47 female–54 male	
Education (years)	68	10.83	1.83	8.00–15.00
Depression[1]	101	16.18	10.78	0.00–45.00
CPG – pain intensity[2]	101	51.19	16.30	10.00–86.67
CPG – disability score	99	38.28	21.86	0.00–80.00
MPI pain intensity[3]	101	3.11	1.13	0.67–5.67
MPI pain interference	101	2.96	1.33	0.20–5.90
MPI – affective distress	101	2.51	1.38	0.00–5.67
MPI – life control	101	3.90	1.17	1.33–6.00
MPI – social support	97	3.38	1.65	0.00–6.00
MPI – total activities	98	2.66	0.95	0.58–4.47

[1]Measured with the German version of the Center for Epidemiologic Studies Depression Scale (Hautzinger & Bailer, 1993). [2]Measured with the German version of the Chronic Pain Grade Scale (Von Korff, Ormel, Keefe, & Dworkin, 1992). [3]Measured with the German version of the West Haven-Yale Multidimensional Pain Inventory (Flor et al., 1990).

chronic back pain (0 = chronic back pain got worse, 1 = chronic back pain did not change, 2 = chronic back pain got better), and to rate the side effects due to this specific pain medication (0 = many side effects, 1 = a few side effects, 2 = no side effects). This part of the questionnaire had been specifically constructed for chronic back pain patients taking into account the most frequently prescribed drugs in the outpatient pain clinic of the Medical Faculty Mannheim, Heidelberg University. The following medications were sampled: paracetamol, ibuprofen, diclofenac, Novalgin® (metamizole), Voltaren® (diclofenac topical gel), transdermal pain patches (e.g., Norspan® or Transtec® (buprenorphine), Durogesic® (fentanyl)), opioids, Tramal®/Tramadol®, Valoron®/Tilidin®, antidepressants (e.g., amitriptyline, citalopram, fluoxetine, imipramine). In question no. 11, patients were able to fill in pain medication that they took but that was not mentioned in the above questions. Three overall scores were computed: mean efficacy of pain medication (calculated as the sum of the second part of the question divided by the number of pain medication that the patient had experience with), experience with side effects of pain medication (calculated as the sum of the third part of the question divided by the number of pain medications that the patient had experience with), and number of pain medications taken (calculated as the sum of the first part of the question).

In addition patients were also asked to complete the BMQ (Horne et al., 1999) and the PMAQ (McCracken et al., 2006).

Thirty-two of the patients underwent an extensive pain interview (Flor & Turk, 2011). Here patients were quizzed about their pain medication use and short- and long-term efficacy of these pain medications. Eight variables were calculated from this interview:

(1) short-term efficacy of non-/minimally invasive pain medication (i.e., oral or percutaneous intake of pain medication; only pharmacologically relevant components);
(2) long-term effectiveness of non-/minimally invasive pain medication (i.e., oral or percutaneous intake of pain medication; only pharmacologically relevant components);
(3) short-term efficacy of invasive treatments (e.g., operations, injections, nerve-resection);
(4) long-term efficacy of invasive treatments (e.g., operations, injections, nerve-resection);
(5) short-term efficacy of every-day treatments (e.g., heating pads, herbal medication, homoeopathic medication, alcohol, prayers, and sports);
(6) long-term efficacy of every-day treatments (e.g., heating pads, herbal medication, homoeopathic medication, alcohol, prayers, and sports);
(7) short-term efficacy of other prescriptions (e.g., massages, physiotherapeutic interventions, sleeping pills, acupuncture, psychotherapy); and
(8) long-term efficacy of other prescriptions (e.g., massages, physiotherapeutic interventions, sleeping pills, acupuncture, psychotherapy).

Additionally, for 38 patients we report the results of a pharmacological placebo in the form of a plaster attached to the patients' back. Patients indicated the extent of the experimental pain on a visual analogue scale, ranging from "0 = no pain" to "100 = worst pain imaginable" before and after the placebo intervention. The placebo response was calculated as the rating after the intervention minus patients' rating before the intervention. Negative numbers thus indicate pain relief, positive numbers pain exacerbation.

The study was conducted in accordance with the Declaration of Helsinki and approved by the Ethics Committee of the Medical Faculty Mannheim of Heidelberg University and the local Ethics Committee of the Medical Board in Hamburg, Germany. All subjects gave their written informed consent to participate in the study and were free to terminate the experiment at any time.

Data Analysis

For the questionnaires and the scales of pain-related attitude and experience, means, standard deviation, and range of the obtained results are reported. The relationships between variables were analyzed using Pearson's correlations. Linear regression was used with a step-wise inclusion and the eight variables from the pain interview. Pearson's correlations were also used for the analysis of the relationship between the attitude and experience data and the placebo response. Group differences were calculated using independent sample t-tests. All calculations were carried out with IBM SPSS Statistics (Version 21).

Results

Data on the BMQ and PMAQ

The scores for the BMQ and PMAQ can be found in Table 2. For the BMQ scores, our sample of chronic back pain patients was quite comparable with the study sample of Horne et al. (1999). For the PMAQ, our patients scored generally higher than the sample of McCracken et al. (2006), indicating that our patients showed more worries/fears regarding medication.

Attitude Toward Pain Medication

For the mean score regarding attitude patients reported a slightly negative attitude ($M = 2.73$, $SD = 0.35$). The means and standard deviations of the individual questions can be found in Table 3. Pain-free controls also had a slightly negative attitude toward pain ($M = 2.53$, $SD = 0.47$). However, they indicated a significantly more positive attitude than pain patients, $t(124) = 3.60$, $p < .001$.

Attitude toward pain medication showed a significant positive correlation with the BMQ General Benefit scale ($r = 0.23$, $p = .023$) but not with any other subscales of the BMQ or with any subscales of the PMAQ.

Table 2. Means, standard deviation, and range of the subscales of the two questionnaires BMQ (Beliefs about Medicine Questionnaire) and PMAQ (Pain Medication Attitude Questionnaire) and data of the original normative samples

Item	*N*	Mean (study sample)	Standard deviation (study sample)	Range (study sample)	Mean and standard deviation (reference sample[1])
BMQ general overuse	101	14.43	2.63	8–20	12.42 (2.76)
BMQ general harm	101	10.51	2.74	4–18	9.86 (2.80)
BMQ specific necessity	100	14.84	5.79	5–25	19.65 (3.92)
BMQ specific concerns	100	13.36	5.34	5–36	14.26 (3.92)
PMAQ addiction	100	5.94	6.18	0–25	1.41 (1.33)
PMAQ need	100	12.21	6.72	0–27	2.81 (1.16)
PMAQ scrutiny	99	8.52	4.96	0–20	1.04 (0.99)
PMAQ side effects	99	10.93	7.86	0–30	1.97 (1.26)
PMAQ tolerance	99	7.62	5.60	0–25	2.18 (1.23)
PMAQ mistrust MDs	99	18.12	6.16	0–31	1.30 (1.12)
PMAQ withdrawal	99	4.98	4.90	0–18	1.80 (1.36)

[1]For the BMQ general medical sample of Horne et al., 1999; for the PMAQ sample form McCracken et al., 2006.

Table 3. Attitude toward pain medication broken down to the single questions that comprise the attitude scale

Item*	Number of subjects	Mean	Standard deviation
1) Amelioration of life due to pain medication	101	2.99	0.69
2) Willingness to put up with side effects	101	2.97	0.78
3) Discontinuation of medication when effective	101	2.93	1.10
4) Belief about harmfulness of pain medication	101	2.69	0.90
5) Willingness to take pain medication	101	2.95	0.89
6) Willingness to bear pain instead of taking pain medication	100	2.68	0.89
7) Pain medication as immediate action	101	1.96	0.81
8) Unwillingness to take pain medication	101	2.67	0.99
Mean attitude score	101	2.73	0.35

*Scale: 1 = do not agree at all, 2 = somewhat disagree, 3 = somewhat agree, 4 = agree fully.

Table 4. Experience with pain medication broken down to the single questions that comprise the experience scale

	N[a]	Mean change of CBP due to medication[+]	Standard deviation	*N*[b]	Mean side effects of medication[++]	Standard deviation
1) Paracetamol	34	1.24	0.50	34	1.67	0.68
2) Ibuprofen	73	1.63	0.49	71	1.65	0.61
3) Diclofenac	56	1.64	0.52	54	1.33	0.70
4) Novalgin® (metamizole)	50	1.51	0.51	49	1.37	0.83
5) Voltaren® (diclofenac topical gel)	63	1.60	0.49	57	1.68	0.54
6) Transdermal pain patches	21	1.50	0.69	18	1.22	0.65
7) Opioids	28	1.86	0.35	28	0.86	0.69
8) Tramal®/Tramadol®	28	1.68	0.48	26	1.31	0.74
9) Valoron®/Tilidin®	21	1.75	0.44	20	1.05	0.83
10) Antidepressants	29	1.28	0.46	27	1.19	0.68

[a]Number of patients reporting having taken the medication, [b]Number of patients reporting side effects of the medication, [+]0 = chronic back pain got worse due to medication, 1 = no change in chronic back pain, 2 = chronic back pain improved due to medication; [++]0 = many side effects, 1 = a few side effects, 2 = no side effects.

Experience With Pain Medication

Patients reported a mean number of 4.07 pain medications (*SD* = 2.21, range = 0.00–9.00) and a mean number of side effects of 1.50 (*SD* = 0.53, range = 0.00–2.00). They rated the mean experience with pain medication as slightly positive (mean = 1.59, *SD* = 0.36, range = 0.75–2.00). The means and standard deviations of the individual questions can be found in Table 4. Pain-free control subjects had a mean experience with pain medication

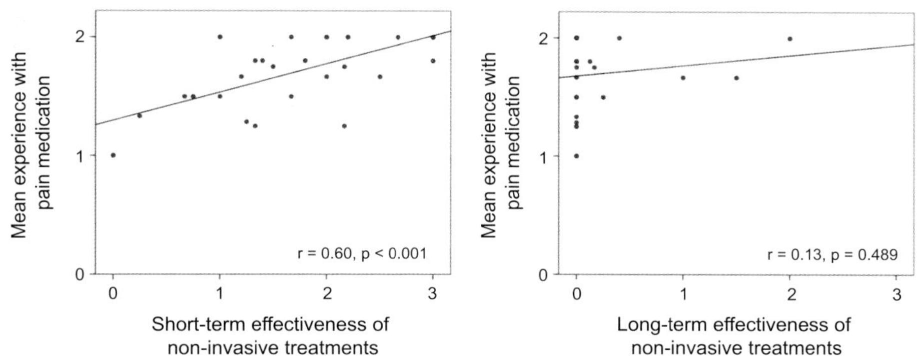

Figure 1. Relationship between efficacy of treatments. Left: correlation of short-term efficacy of noninvasive treatments (assessed via a pain interview) with questionnaire score of mean experience with pain medication. Right: nonsignificant correlation of long-term effectiveness of noninvasive treatments (assessed via a pain interview) with the score of mean experience with pain medication. Higher scores indicate positive experience with pain medication (i.e., high efficacy).

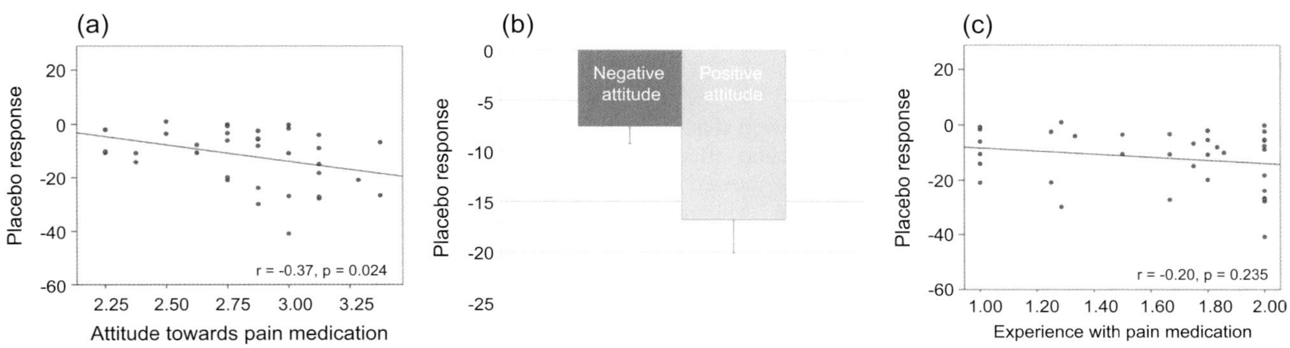

Figure 2. Placebo response and attitude and experience. (a) Significant negative correlation between attitude scores (small numbers indicating a negative attitude, larger numbers indicating a positive attitude) and the placebo response (large negative numbers indicating a large pain reduction, smaller negative numbers a smaller pain reduction and positive numbers a pain exacerbation). (b) Significant differences between the size of the placebo response and the attitude (p = 0.013). (c) No correlation between experience scores and the placebo response.

of 1.95 (SD = 0.12), indicating a more positive experience with pain medication compared to the patients, $t(115) = -4.36$, $p < .001$.

Experience with pain medication showed no significant correlations with any of the BMQ or PMAQ subscales.

When only the 32 patients, who additionally underwent the extensive interview, were analyzed using a step-wise inclusion approach, the mean experience score could be predicted by the variable short-term efficacy of non-/minimally invasive pain medication (i.e., oral or percutaneous intake of pain medication; only pharmacologically relevant components) (R = 0.63, R-Square = 0.40, p = .001). Short-term efficacy of noninvasive treatments also correlated significantly with the mean experience score (r = 0.68, $p < .001$), long-term efficacy of noninvasive treatments showed no significant correlation (r = 0.24, p = .49), see Figure 1.

Placebo Response

Patients reported a mean placebo response of −6.53 (SD = 13.41, range = −50.00 to +30.00; paired sample t-test$_{\text{pre-post}}$: $t(37) = 6.77$, $p < .001$), indicating that our pharmacological placebo significantly reduced the experimental pain. Eight patients (21%) showed an exacerbation of pain due to the placebo intervention, 5 patients (13%) reported no change, and 25 patients (66%) could be classified as placebo responders. There was a negative correlation between the placebo response and patients' attitude toward pain medication ($r = -0.37$, p = .024); see Figure 2a. Patients with a more positive attitude displayed a larger placebo response to experimental pain stimuli. Additionally, the patients were classified for their attitude toward medication score into two subgroups by using a median split (median attitude = 2.88, scores < 2.88

[n = 16] indicating a more negative attitude, scores > 2.88 [n = 14] indicating a more positive attitude). A comparison of the two groups showed a significant difference. Patients with a positive attitude had a significantly larger placebo response than patients with a negative attitude, $t(28) = 2.65$, $p = .013$; see Figure 2b. Linear regression showed that the mean attitude score moderately predicted the size of the placebo response ($R = 0.37$, R-Square = 0.14, $p = .027$).

There was no significant correlation between the experience with pain medication score and the placebo response ($p = .24$, see Figure 2c) nor a significant group difference ($p = .21$). However, this could be due to the skewed distribution of the experience score. This score had a possible range of 0 (negative experiences) to 2 (positive experiences). Twelve patients had a mean score of 2, six patients a score of 1, and no patient indicated scores below 1 (see Figure 2c for the distribution). Hence, our sample comprised mainly patients with a neutral and positive experience and not patients with negative experience.

Discussion

Using the scale of pain-related attitude we showed that a negative attitude was related to a smaller placebo effect in a clinical sample. Chronic back pain patients showed a slightly negative attitude toward medication whereas pain-free control subjects showed a significantly more positive attitude. Regarding the effects of attitude toward medication on the placebo response, we could show that the mean attitude score explained 14% of the variance of the placebo response of patients. Experience with pain medication and the placebo response did not correlate significantly. This might be due to the fact that patients with extremely negative experience did not participate in our study on pharmacological placebos and we could thus not capture the full range of the scale. Patients reported a slightly positive experience with pain medication and, as expected, healthy pain free control subjects reported an even stronger positive experience with pain medication. Additionally, experience with pain medication could be predicted using the pain interview (short-term efficacy of non-/minimally invasive pain medication) with an explained variance of 40%.

So far, the only suitable way to assess the patients' experience with pain medication was through a comprehensive interview (Flor & Turk, 2011). Our items to assess experience with pain medication and the information obtained from the interview regarding noninvasive short-term effects of medication correlated significantly ($r = 0.65$, $p < .001$). The correlation with long-term effects of medication was not significant. This suggests that patients refer more to the short-term effects of medication than any possible long-term effects. This is, however, not surprising. First, effective pain medication would decrease patients' pain to a level where they would no longer have participated in our study. And second, there is no effective long-term pain medication for chronic back pain up to date. Experience with pain medication showed a moderate positive correlation with the number of medications tried, indicating that patients seem to achieve some sort of endpoint ($r = 0.41$, $p < .001$). If they lower their expectations toward the pain medication after many unsuccessful trials of medication or by finally obtaining the best suitable medication for their individual pain problem cannot be answered by our study.

As we have pointed out, experience and attitude have been identified as two modulating factors in experimental placebo analgesia in human subjects (Benedetti, 2012; Benedetti & Amanzio, 2013; Bingel, Schoell, & Buchel, 2007; Colloca, Sigaudo, & Benedetti, 2008; Finniss & Benedetti, 2005; Pollo & Benedetti, 2009; Voudouris et al., 1990). Capturing patients' attitude toward and experience with pain medication can lead to a better understanding of the mechanisms involved in the development of a placebo response in chronic pain patients. Further research should include measurements of attitude toward and experience with pain medication in studies of placebo analgesia.

Acknowledgments

This research was funded by grants by the German Research Foundation (FOR 1328/1) to H. F. (Fl 156/33-1) and R. K. (Kl 1350/3-1).

References

Benedetti, F. (2012). Placebo-induced improvements: How therapeutic rituals affect the patient's brain. *Journal of Acupuncture and Meridian Studies, 5*, 97–103.

Benedetti, F., & Amanzio, M. (2013). Mechanisms of the placebo response. *Pulmonary Pharmacology & Therapeutics, 26*, 520–523.

Bingel, U., Schoell, E., & Buchel, C. (2007). Imaging pain modulation in health and disease. *Current Opinions in Neurology, 20*, 424–431.

Colloca, L., & Benedetti, F. (2006). How prior experience shapes placebo analgesia. *Pain, 124*, 126–133.

Colloca, L., Sigaudo, M., & Benedetti, F. (2008). The role of learning in nocebo and placebo effects. *Pain, 136*, 211–218.

Finniss, D. G., & Benedetti, F. (2005). Mechanisms of the placebo response and their impact on clinical trials and clinical practice. *Pain, 114*, 3–6.

Finniss, D. G., Kaptchuk, T. J., Miller, F., & Benedetti, F. (2010). Biological, clinical, and ethical advances of placebo effects. *Lancet, 375*, 686–695.

Flor, H., Rudy, T. E., Birbaumer, N., Streit, B., & Schugens, M. M. (1990). Zur Anwendbarkeit des West Haven-Yale Multidimensional Pain Inventory im deutschen Sprachraum [On the applicability of the West Haven-Yale Multidimensional Pain Inventory in German-speaking areas]. *Der Schmerz, 4*, 82–87.

Flor, H., & Turk, D. C. (2011). *Chronic pain: An integrated biobehavioral approach*. Seattle, WA: IASP Press.

Hautzinger, M., & Bailer, M. (1993). *Allgemeine Depressions Skalà (ADS)* [General depression scale]. Weinheim, Germany: Beltz Test.
Horne, R., Weinmann, J., & Hankins, M. (1999). The beliefs about medicines questionnaire: The development and evaluation of a new method for assessing the cognitive representation of medication. *Psychology & Health, 14*, 1–24.
McCracken, L. M., Hoskins, J., & Eccleston, C. (2006). Concerns about medication and medication use in chronic pain. *Journal of Pain, 7*, 726–734.
Pollo, A., & Benedetti, F. (2009). The placebo response: Neurobiological and clinical issues of neurological relevance. *Progress in Brain Research, 175*, 283–294.
Von Korff, M., Ormel, J., Keefe, F. J., & Dworkin, S. F. (1992). Grading the severity of chronic pain. *Pain, 50*, 133–149.
Voudouris, N. J., Peck, C. L., & Coleman, G. (1990). The role of conditioning and verbal expectancy in the placebo response. *Pain, 43*, 121–128.

Sandra Kamping

Department of Cognitive and Clinical Neuroscience
Central Institute of Mental Health
Square J5
68159 Mannheim
Germany
Tel. +49 621 1701-6342
Fax + 49 621 1703-6305
E-mail sandra.kamping@zi-mannheim.de

Call for Papers

"New Directions in Reactance Theory"

A Topical Issue of the *Zeitschrift für Psychologie*

Guest Editors: Sandra Sittenthaler, Eva Jonas, Eva Traut-Mattausch
(University of Salzburg, Austria), and Jeff Greenberg
(University of Arizona, Tucson, AZ, USA)

Psychological reactance theory (Brehm, 1966; Brehm & Brehm, 1981) is one of the most popular social psychological theories explaining how people respond to threats to their free behaviors. Despite a wealth of studies mainly investigating the effects of reactance, there is a need to better understand issues still outstanding and exciting questions concerning the process activated by the motivation to restore one's own freedom and the consequences of reactance. In his last review paper before his death in 2009, Brehm himself pointed toward several gaps in reactance research (Miron & Brehm, 2006). Brehm and his colleagues recommended not only to continue to investigate the basic theoretical assumptions but also to explore the physiology of reactance, the phenomenon of "vicarious reactance," and implications of reactance for real-world phenomena. This topical issue of the *Zeitschrift für Psychologie* aims at shedding some light on reactance processes and their consequences.

The topical issue invites submissions of empirical papers dedicated to new reactance theory findings. Contributions that focus on, but are not limited to, the following topics are particularly welcome:

- Further developments of reactance theory.
- Vicarious reactance.
- Energizing and activating effects of reactance.
- Real reactance behavior.
- Intervention studies.
- Neurocognitive approaches to reactance theory.

We invite scholars to submit their abstracts on potential papers electronically to: Dr. Sandra Sittenthaler (Sandra.Sittenthaler2@sbg.ac.at).

How to submit: Interested authors should submit a letter of intent including: (1) a working title for the manuscript, (2) names, affiliations, and contact information for all authors, and (3) an abstract of no more than 500 words detailing the content of the proposed manuscript.

There is a *two-stage submissions process*. Initially, interested authors are requested to submit only abstracts of their proposed papers. Authors of the selected abstracts will then be invited to submit full papers. All papers will undergo blind peer review.

Deadline for submission of abstracts is October 15, 2014.
Deadline for submission of full papers is February 15, 2015.

The journal seeks to maintain a short turnaround time, with the final version of the accepted papers being due by May, 15, 2015. The topical issue will be published as issue 4 (2015).

For additional information, please contact any of the guest editors:

Dr. Sandra Sittenthaler (Sandra.Sittenthaler2@sbg.ac.at),
Prof. Dr. Eva Jonas (Eva.Jonas@sbg.ac.at),
Prof. Dr. Eva Traut-Mattausch (Eva.Traut-Mattausch@sbg.ac.at),
Prof. Dr. Jeff Greenberg (jeff@email.arizona.edu).

About the Journal

The *Zeitschrift für Psychologie*, founded in 1890, is the oldest psychology journal in Europe and the second oldest in the world. One of the founding editors was Hermann Ebbinghaus. Since 2007 it is published in English and devoted to publishing topical issues that provide state-of-the-art reviews of current research in psychology.

For detailed author guidelines, please see the journal's website at www.hogrefe.com/journals/zfp/.

References

Brehm, J. W. (1966). *A theory of psychological reactance*. New York, NY: Academic Press.
Brehm, S. S., & Brehm, J. W. (1981). *Psychological reactance. A theory of freedom and control*. New York, NY: Academic Press.
Miron, A. M., & Brehm, J. W. (2006). Reactance theory – 40 years later. *Zeitschrift für Sozialpsychologie, 37*, 9–18.

DOI: 10.1027/2151-2604/a000174